On Fire for God

Books
by the Same Author

Companion Volume

A Fistful of Heroes:
Great Reformers and Evangelists

The Cambridge Seven
Hudson Taylor and Maria
Moody Without Sankey
Billy Graham
George Whitefield
Wilberforce
The Siberian Seven
The Apostle: A life of Paul
The Master: A life of Jesus
Amazing Grace: John Newton's Story
Shaftesbury: The Poor Man's Earl
John Wesley

and other books

On Fire for God

Great Missionary Pioneers

John Pollock

OM
LIT

OPERATION
MOBILIZATION
LITERATURE
MINISTRY

*Bringing hope
to the nations*

STAR BOOKS
LONDON

STAR BOOKS, 99 Marlow Road, London SE20 7XW

Operation Mobilization Literature Minsitry, P.O. Box 1047,
Waynesboro, Georgia 30830-2047, U.S.A.

First published by Marshall Pickering, part of the
HarperCollins Publishing Group

This edition 1995

ISBN (UK): 1 899353 00 3
ISBN (USA): 1 844543 01 4

Printed in England by Cox & Wyman Ltd, Cardiff Rd,
Reading RG1 8EX

To
A.J. Broomhall

*Missionary Pioneer
and
Biographer*

Contents

Preface

In the last years of the eighteenth century the Christian faith was virtually confined to Europe and parts of the Americas, with small pockets surviving from an earlier age in North Africa and Asia.

Two hundred years later almost every country of the world has a Christian church, and the faith grows fastest in Africa and China. Under God, a prime cause of this vast expansion was the willingness of men and women to leave the security of Europe or North America to become pioneers, far from home, often at the end of a long sea voyage to a little known land.

I have traced a pattern of them across the earth, selecting a few to represent the multitude. Some were household names; three were martyrs. They all differed from each other in character and achievement but their dedication shames a softer age. And the subject of my final sketch, "Lord Apostol", long forgotten in his own country, is perhaps the most relevant of all; for his life story is a key to the events unfolding in Russia in the last decade of the twentieth century.

Rose Ash   John Pollock
Devonshire

Acknowledgements

Eleven of these sketches first appeared in either the British magazine *Crusade* (now *Leadership Today*) or the American magazine *World Vision*, and were previously published as a collection in the United States by Word Books under the title *Victims of the Long March*. I thank the editors and publishers for their willingness to allow them to be reprinted.

"The Lame Cow's Friend" appeared long ago in a different form in my story of the Zenana Bible and Medical Mission, *Shadows Fall Apart* (Hodder and Stoughton). "Stroke Oar", "Test Cricketer" and "A Torch is Lit" are abridged from *The Cambridge Seven* (InterVarsity Press, 1955, Marshall Pickering, 1985) which is now out of print; I particularly welcome the opportunity to keep the Cambridge Seven in the public mind. Some of the material in "Lord Apostol" was published in my book of 1964, *The Christians From Siberia* (Hodder and Stoughton). I am grateful to these two publishers for allowing such pioneers a new lease of life. "Lassie Queen of Calabar" and "The Good Gossips of Gobi" are published for the first time.

As any sketch writer should, I gladly acknowledge the help of biographies and autobiographies, old and more recent, and would especially pay tribute to James Buchan's *The Expendable Mary Slessor* (St Andrew's Press, 1980) and to W. J. Platt's *Three*

Women (Hodder and Stoughton, 1964). Also to the missionary-travel books of Mildred Cable with Francesca French, still highly enjoyable more than thirty years after the death of the authors.

The sketches of Rosalie Harvey, Hudson Taylor, and the Cambridge Seven are based on my own research in the manuscript sources.

White Man's Grave

1
Lassie Queen of Calabar

Mary Slessor 1848–1915

The chattering stopped. Wives, their black bodies fattened according to custom, and widows, emaciated according to custom, moved closer together as a little white woman strode into the centre of the palaver where the chiefs of the tribe were seated in judgement on two young wives. The people of the village watched in wonder as the chiefs, who scorned women as mere chattels of men, rose in respect for Mary Slessor, already widely known up the creeks of Calabar as "Ma".

She wore a shapeless, sleeveless garment, not the formal long-sleeved dress which was normal for white women in the tropics in 1882; and her head was uncovered except for her shock of close cropped red hair, for she refused to wear the sun helmet which the doctors insisted was vital for Europeans. And since she always ate African food, and slept on the floor among the wives, all the village of Ibaka loved their guest, for her laughter and jokes, and her medicine chest, and because she taught about God.

Today she was grave. Two of a chief's wives had crept out of the wives' compound and had been caught in the hut of a young man, thus breaking tribal law.

Two others were held as accomplices; and a palaver of
chiefs had sentenced all four to a hundred lashes each
with the crocodile hide whip – a virtual sentence of
death. Mary had heard at once and gone to the head of
the tribe, Chief Okon, the man who had invited her to
visit their village from her base upriver at Old Town.

She urged him not to have the girls flogged. He was
amazed. She persisted. At length he said, "Ma, it be a
proper big palaver but if you say we must not flog we
must listen to you as our mother and our guest. But
they will say that God's word be no good if it destroy
the law's power to punish evildoers." He had agreed
to delay the sentence and reconvene the palaver. Thus
Mary Slessor could now address the tribal court.

First she turned to the girls and addressed them
in fluent Efik. Among Europeans she spoke broad
Scots, but she had absorbed the local language so
fully that every inflection and grunt made her sound
almost like a native.

She scolded the girls for abusing their master's trust.
"Though God's word teaches men to be merciful it
does not pass over sin. I cannot shield you from
punishment. Ask God to keep you in future so that
your behaviour is not a reproach to yourselves or to
the word of God which you have learned."

The village elders looked pleased; but now she
turned on them. "It is *you* who are to blame!", she
cried. "It is your custom of many wives to a man
which is a disgrace!" Her blue eyes flashing, she
lashed the men with her tongue. "It is a disgrace
to you and a cruel injustice to these helpless girls.
Only sixteen years old, full of fun and frolic yet
you shut them up in a hut. It is a blot on your

manhood! Obedience to your sort of laws is not worth having!"

She sat down. The palaver debated the case until at last the sentence of each was reduced to ten strokes of the whip, and no salt to be rubbed in the wounds, and no mutilation to follow.

Mary went into the hut to prepare bandages and ointments. Soon she heard the whistle and thud of the whip, the screams of the first victim and the laughter of those who watched. A naked, bleeding girl ran in, shivering in her agony. Mary washed and dressed the wounds and gave her a dose of laudanum to send her into an uneasy sleep. Soon came the next, screaming in shock and pain.

Some days later Mary Slessor boarded the royal canoe for the homeward journey through the forest. She knew that her visit had only thrown into sharper relief the cruelties and miseries, and the spiritual hunger, of a land scarcely touched as yet by the Gospel and kindness of Christ.

.   .   .   .   .

Mary Slessor was then thirty-four. She had been in Calabar for only six years, including a furlough to recover her health, for she was frequently down with the fevers which caused the death of numerous missionaries in "the White Man's Grave" of West Africa. Mary Slessor always survived.

She had been brought up to hardship and poverty in the slums of Dundee, one of the many children of an alcoholic father and a devout mother who had a special interest in the Free Church of Scotland's

Calabar mission. This had been founded in 1849 by
Scottish missionaries from Jamaica, at the urging of
elderly ex-slaves who had been abducted from the
region before the abolition of the slave trade, and
who well knew that Calabar was a land of violence
and sorrow.

Mary had worked for fifteen years as a weaver in a
Dundee factory. At first she was wild, until converted
to Christ through the words of an old woman who
terrified her with fear of hell fire – a method which
Mary herself, though grateful, would never use on
a soul. She became a skilled Sunday school teacher
among the roughest boys and girls in the slums, until
the inward call to Calabar became too insistent to
resist.

The Foreign Mission committee sent her to Edinburgh for three months to improve her education
and increase her experience, until at last, in 1876,
she reached Calabar at the age of twenty-eight.

She found swamps and forests and broad rivers;
a land of great natural beauty, with kingfishers and
cranes and parrots; with elephants and leopards in
great numbers which, with poisonous snakes on
land and crocodiles in the rivers, made travel a
hazard. And always the myriads of insects, especially
mosquitoes, which had not yet been identified as the
carriers of the malaria which was so often fatal.

Except for small settlements on the estuaries, where
white traders bought and exported palm oil, Calabar
was unpacified by any colonial power. Britain claimed
it as a "sphere of influence" but had not attempted to
annex or control; inter-tribal warfare and the legacy of
the Atlantic slave trade, abolished only seventy years

earlier, had made the people of Calabar a byword for savagery and degradation. Brutal and arbitrary justice was administered by a secret council called Egbo; and if a chief died, his funeral required human sacrifices of many of his slaves and some of his wives.

Brought up to hardship and life among the poor, Mary Slessor soon felt at home. She quickly grew impatient with the formal European ways of the Scottish missionaries who had survived the climate. She recognized their sincerity and courage but was determined to understand the African's outlook. She soon realized that the men and women of the forest and river banks were instinctively religious, gripped by witchcraft and spirit worship; and that many of the cruellest customs were imposed by religion, a religion which knew nothing of the love of God.

Twins must be strangled or thrown alive into the forest, because one of them was begotten by the devil in a secret mating. Missionaries had done their best to teach otherwise, but Mary was willing to hurry at once on news of twins to save them from death, even if it meant walking a forest path at night, with the terrifying sounds of animals and night birds, and the vampire bats flying. She rescued twins and orphan babies – who would have been thrown out too – and always seemed to have a family of them around her: two of those whom she adopted, Jean and David, grew up to be her devoted companions and fellow workers for God.

The senior missionaries patiently put up with Mary being late for meals, and running races with the blacks, and even climbing trees with the boys if

she thought it would help to open their hearts to
Christ. At last the mission allowed her to live on
her own in a poor part of the town. She could now
eat as the Africans did (except that she liked a nice
cup of tea whenever she could get it), and soon
had an extraordinary influence, especially among the
slaves.

It was while living in Old Town, by herself, except
for her rescued babies, that she had visited Okon's
village and saved the lives of the young wives who
had been sentenced to a hundred lashes. On her way
back in Okon's canoe she had nearly been lost in a
violent storm in the estuary. She huddled terrified
beside one of Okon's large wives, but when the crew
panicked, the drummer stopped beating, the crew
stopped paddling and the canoe tossed aimlessly,
Mary lost her temper and yelled at the drummer to
start again. The paddlers recovered their rhythm and
brought the canoe to an island, where they all clung
to an overhanging mangrove tree until the storm died
down.

Mary's great desire, however, was to settle up-
country among a tribe of powerful physique named
the Okoyong. Two senior Scotsmen of the mission had
visited them and seen the violence of their ways, and
were not disposed to allow Mary to venture there. But
in 1884 the British declared a Protectorate. Just four
years later the mission leaders allowed Mary Slessor
to visit the Okoyong to see whether they would accept
her.

"Like all isolated peoples," she wrote, "they are
conservative and independent. They are brave, almost fierce, war-loving, and as reckless of their

own lives as they are of others'." She made three preliminar visits to their biggest village, Ekenge, and its neighbourhood.

At last the Okoyong allowed her to settle. When she arrived the tribe had gone off for a week of riot around a funeral. Only a few weeks earlier, she learned from the head chief's sister, Eme Eta, they had celebrated a funeral by strangling the dead man's four wives, together with eight slave men, eight slave women, five girls and five boys.

Mary began to hold services every day, attended mostly at first by women, children and slaves. Almost every other minute was spent in treating patients in a village which had never known modern medicine. In the evenings the tribe would give itself up to drink. "*Everybody* drinks", she wrote. "I have lain down at night knowing that not a sober man and hardly a sober woman was within miles of me."

Then she saved the life of a chief's wife by walking with her medicines eight hours through pitiless rain in response to an urgent call; and by saving the woman she saved those who would have been human sacrifices at her death. The tribe began to recognize that their visitor's God had power. Mary herself experienced, over and over again, the power of God through prayer. She started a little garden so that she could pray as she hoed, for it was difficult to pray in the noise of her hut, crowded with visitors, village cats, cockroaches and wandering chickens. And her adopted son, Daniel Slessor, once an abandoned orphan, remembered how she would stand in "forest clearings looking up, her blue eyes fixed steadfastly above, her lips moving . . . . She was praying to God for help, strength, courage and resource."

One day a valuable and beautiful slave girl, bought from another tribe, went to the hut of a young male slave, with whom she had fallen in love, and tried to persuade him to run away with her; but he knew that they were sure to be caught and die a terrible death. He refused. She went into the forest and hanged herself.

The young man was summarily tried by the village council and sentenced to be flogged and then executed. Mary at once protested that this was unfair: he had refused the girl. The chiefs retorted that he was being punished for bewitching her. "What evidence have you?", demanded Mary. They replied that evidence was not needed: since the girl had entered his hut, he must have bewitched her.

Mary would have none of it. A court of law must not convict without evidence, she insisted.

At that the village council erupted with rage. The chiefs and the watching freemen leaped and yelled at Mary. They waved knives and guns, and threw dust, and glared at her. Mary was frightened. To show fear might cause her own death, and if she gave in and allowed the man to die she would lose all her growing influence. She glared back, and soon her quick Scots temper took hold of her; she was so angry that all fear went, and she stood there, blue eyes blazing under her red hair, until suddenly the storm subsided. The chiefs sat down, certain that this was no mere woman. As she once wrote in her Bible, "God and one is a majority."

They agreed to let her argue the slave's case and at last they compromised: he should be flogged but not killed. Knowing she could go no further she thanked them for their clemency, to save them face.

But they carried out the flogging, once a day for three days, close to her hut, so that she heard the whip and his screams. They gave him no food or water, and set guards so that she could not reach him. After three days they released him from chains and she nursed him back to health.

A few nights later the yard near her house was the scene of a drunken orgy to entertain visiting guests, with the men noisily taking their pleasure on slave girls, willing or not. Mary wrote: "If I did not know that my Saviour is near me, I would go out of my mind."

.   .   .   .   .

In 1891 the British set up a system of vice-consular justice in Calabar. Mary Slessor had established such an influence over the Okoyong that Sir Claude Macdonald, the consul-general, made her a vice-consul, the first woman to be so appointed in the British Empire. Justice emphatically was done, though her court could be a little eccentric. One British official found her in a rocking chair with a baby in her lap, listening to litigants and witnesses, all treating her with great respect. "Suddenly she jumped up with an angry growl." The baby was transferred and she hurried to the door, "where a hulking, overdressed native stood. In a moment she seized him by the scruff of the neck, boxed his ears and hustled him out into

the yard." The man "a local monarch of sorts", had
disobeyed her and been forbidden her court until he
apologized.

Yet on her infrequent furloughs to Scotland, when
Mary Slessor was expected to speak at missionary
meetings, she was overcome. "I am suffering tortures
of fear", she wrote before one meeting, "and yet why
is it I cannot rest in Him? If He sends me work, surely
He will help me to deliver His message, and to do it
for His glory. He has never failed me before." Nor
did He fail her: on that occasion, as often, she gave
an extempore address which enthralled and moved
her audience.

After fifteen years among the Okoyong she could
rejoice in a small church of strong Christian believers
but a widened acceptance of Christian values, helped
by the law and order brought by the British Empire.
Human sacrifice had stopped at funerals; floggings
were no longer at the whim of a master or husband;
the dreaded ordeal by poison bean – by which guilt
or innocence, death or life, were determined by
chance or by the manipulation of a witch doctor –
was stopped, though slavery still continued.

.   .   .   .   .   .

For years the Scottish mission did not find any one to
replace Mary. Those Scotswomen who came to help
her were inclined to give up, through illness or despair
of the conditions. Once she became engaged to marry
another missionary, much younger than she was, but
when his health prevented his return to Calabar the
engagement quietly lapsed.

At last arrangements were made which would free Mary Slessor to go farther inland, to the sorrow of all the Okoyong. She set her sights on the Aro, a tribe which was the terror of Calabar. She had met several of their chiefs when they visited Ekenge. Deep in their territory was a famous shrine which attracted many pilgrims from other tribes. Few returned home: the Aro took their offerings, killed them or sold them into slavery. The shrine's fame ensured a steady supply of victims until the British authorities determined on a military expedition to pacify the country and end the murders.

Just then, Mary had planned to visit the Aro. By a mischance which she saw as a providence, she missed the launch; when she hailed the next, on the following day, she found the British commander on board. He treated her with great respect and when they landed at the Aro's principal town, she bareheaded in her shapeless dress and he in his immaculate uniform and sun helmet, he was most impressed that her Aro friends crowded round to greet her.

It was the Aro who gave her the title by which she became known throughout the West Coast of Africa: *Eka kpukpro Owo*, "Mother of All The Peoples". As the British built roads and opened up the country, little Mary Slessor, with her laughter and her prayers and her hot temper, had more influence than any government officer. Once she spent an entire furlough, with the reluctant permission of her home committee, in travelling deeper inland on her own responsibility, teaching and using her medicine chest, and opening the way for the less adventurous to follow.

As the High Commissioner of Nigeria said in 1909: "Miss Slessor can go where no white man can go. She can sway the people when we cannot sway them." She grew old and weak but no less of a legend on the Coast, and was still at work. "My life is one daily, hourly, record of answered prayer . . . for guidance given marvellously, for errors and dangers averted, for enmity to the Gospel subdued, for food provided at the exact hour needed, for everything that goes to make up my life and my poor service, I can testify with a full and often wonder-stricken awe that I believe God answers prayer, I know God answers prayer."

She died, aged sixty-six, in January 1915, among the Africans she loved. The strong church of Nigeria honours her memory and so does Scotland: when Queen Elizabeth II first visited Calabar, she laid a wreath, at her own express wish, on Mary Slessor's grave.

2
Left in Lagos

Rowland V. Bingham 1870–1943

Sitting at the back of a newly opened church in Toronto in the early eighteen-nineties, a young man heard the great missionary statesman, A. J. Gordon, deliver his famous lectures on the Holy Spirit in Missions. Before the series ended the young listener, Rowland V. Bingham, was praying that the Spirit would call him to serve in some distant, lonely corner of the earth.

He went on with his obscure pastorate in the countryside near Toronto. The months passed without a clear answer to his prayer. Then he happened to address a small morning meeting in the city, where an elderly lady with a distinct Scottish accent invited him home for lunch, introducing herself as a Mrs Gowans, a widow. During and after lunch she told him of her son Walter, who had been certain that he was called to take the Gospel to the neediest country he could find. He had pored over maps and statistics until one vast area in Africa had impressed itself on him as almost totally without Christian witness.

From coast to coast, south of the Sahara and north of the rain forests, lay a great, populated belt known in the nineties as the Sudan. Its eastern regions had been wrested by the fanatical Muslim Mahdi from the Anglo-Egyptian rule of General Gordon, murdered at Khartoum seven years before. The French were pushing into its northern-western area, the British were probing from the Gold Coast (Ghana) and up the Niger from Lagos, but almost all the land lay under the rule of slave-raiding Muslim kings or animist tribal chieftains. Before Rowland Bingham left Mrs Gowans, he knew in his heart that he must join Walter Gowans to penetrate the Sudan with the message of the Lord Jesus.

On a fare scraped together by his farmer friends, and with a college contemporary of Gowans', Tom Kent, whom he met in New York, Bingham sailed to England. Gowans had gone ahead, since the mighty British Empire, on which the sun never set, was the colonial power in the region, and it was a British missionary board who must send them. But, like Hudson Taylor when he tried to persuade existing societies to evangelize inland China, Gowans, Bingham and Kent met total refusal for inland Sudan: money was too short, they were told, and the climate was a killer.

The three young men decided to go ahead on their own; they had just enough money to reach Lagos, and the Lord would provide from there. On 4th December 1893, they were anchored off this fever-haunted port, which had as yet no harbour for big ships. Missionaries of the three societies which were working on the coast befriended them to the extent of introducing a tough old trader who rented them a home and, rough sinner as he was, went far beyond the claims of business to help them. But as for going inland, the three North Americans were told they were mad.

Rowland Bingham fell ill with the dreaded malaria which carried off so many in the "White Man's Grave". There was no known cure at that date, and at sunset the doctor sent a message to the Anglican mission home: he could not last the night. The newly arrived bishop, a burly New Zealander named Joseph Hill, came across to pray with Bingham, then gathered the missionaries to special prayer on his behalf. "Do you believe", he asked one of them as they rose from their knees, "that we are going to receive that for which we have asked?"

"I do!" she replied. "I believe that young man is going to be raised up." And he was; but less than a week later Bishop Hill and his wife were both dead of yellow fever, he in the afternoon and she at midnight; of all the party of ten he had brought out only one survived.

When Bingham was strong enough to work again, he and his companions resolved that it was high time to leave for the far interior, for the central Sudan which, Gowan said, was closed only because no one would open the door. They sold almost all their belongings, including their watches, yet still had not enough to pay porters and boatmen – until the mail steamer arrived carrying a gift of $500 from a servant girl called Mary Jones: she had been left a legacy and sent it all to this new, untried, unnamed mission, together with a smaller amount which her mistress added.

By now Gowans, Kent and Bingham had realized that one of them must be left in Lagos to arrange for the despatch up-country of further supplies, for they had no field secretary or committee: the Lagos missionaries, in the kindest possible way, had washed their hands of them, yet they could not live in the interior without trade goods with which to barter, for money was unknown. Unless they engaged porters to carry rolls of calico and sacks of beads, knives, and other odds and ends highly regarded by the tribes, they would be reduced to beggary. Until they could establish a mission station, grow crops and breed cattle, they must depend on more trade goods sent from the coast.

Raymond Bingham, as the convalescent, was the obvious choice to remain behind, however disappointed he might be that he would as yet only see the Sudan interior by the eye of faith and prayer. Gowans and Kent waved goodbye and disappeared up the Niger River, beyond the invisible line which marked the frontier of Lagos Colony, into the distant north. They could not know that they were several years too early: both the pacification, which created Nigeria and ended the tyranny of slave-rading emirs, and the momentous discovery of the cause of malaria lay only a little in the future, but that little meant death.

Gowans and Kent reached a town about six hundred miles from Lagos. Its chief, a fetish worshipper, welcomed them partly because he hoped for a white man's protection from the powerful Moslem emirs whose armies ranged at will. Gowans decided to settle and begin preaching, using his newly acquired, little-tried facility in Hausa, the language most widely used in West Africa. Tom Kent set off to bring up further supplies of trade goods from the coast.

He had not been gone many days when the war drums sounded, the women and children ran screaming into the square, and the men rounded up their stunted cattle and drove them behind the walls of thorn and timber. A Muslim emir was approaching on a slave raid. For two weeks Gowans lived the life of the besieged, his health rapidly worsening, until the town fell to assault while the thatched circular huts went up in flames. The emir enslaved the survivors and drove off their cattle. He offered elegant courtesies to the white man but appropriated his trade goods, cannily offering slaves in payment, knowing they would be refused.

Gowans, expelled, reduced to penury, desperately weak, died of malaria on the way back to the coast.

Kent was ignorant of this tragedy when he reached Lagos after an appalling journey. Bingham nursed him back to health, and accompanied him as far inland as he could go while maintaining their contact with Lagos. Tom Kent went forward to rejoin Gowans – and did so literally, for he too died of malaria, a year and four days after the three young men had landed.

In 1895 Raymond Bingham, the last of the three, returned to North America to find reinforcement and to put the "Sudan Interior Mission", as it was eventually named, on a secure footing. He did not manage to advance on the Sudan again for five years, but in that time he had gained further experience in pastorate and hospital, had won a wife, formed a Mission Council – with flimsy enough finance – and sailed joyfully in 1900 with two other young men.

They landed; the Lagos missionaries were as adamant as before that this was a fool's errand. And when

Bingham once more, within three weeks, developed
malaria and was told it was a choice of death in Lagos
or survival by going back on the steamer which had
brought him, they seemed proved right. "It would
have been easier for me, perhaps," wrote Bingham
in his autobiography, "had I died in Africa, for
on that homeward journey I died another death.
Everything seemed to have failed, and when, while
I was gradually regaining strength in Britain, a fateful
cable reached me with word that my two companions
were arriving shortly, I went through the darkest
period of my life.'

The two companions had been persuaded to give
up by the Lagos missionaries – and disappeared into
oblivion.

Thus, seven years after Bingham had set out with
such sure hopes from Mrs Gowans' parlour, his
mission was a mere mockery. But Mrs Gowans'
response to her son's death had been: 'I would
rather have had Walter go out to the Sudan and die
there all alone, than have him home, disobeying his
Lord.' And Raymond Bingham, too, determined to
continue to obey, whether it led to ridicule or death.

Most of his Council urged the disbanding of this
Sudan Interior Mission that never was. One member
backed Bingham. And four more young men offered.
This time he sent them to healthier parts to learn the
language before they all went to Lagos. Furthermore,
he had met Frederick Lugard, who had recently
defeated the slaver emirs and was on his way back
to the central Sudan to form the peaceful protectorate
of Nigeria. Lord Lugard, as he became, admired
young Bingham and did all he could to encourage

the missionaries. On his advice they made their first home away from the river valleys to avoid the mosquito for the short time remaining before quinine stopped malaria being a fatal disease.

The next seven years saw a growing Mission, one or two deaths – and no conversions whatever. But when Bingham died in 1943, the international, interdenominational Sudan Interior Mission was already numerically one of the largest, with strong national churches growing around it. Today, right across from West Africa to Ethiopia, despite civil wars, persecutions and the difficulties inevitable in a rapidly changing world, these churches represent a powerful witness to Jesus Christ. The printing press which Bingham had founded pours out Christian literature. The voice of Radio Station ELWA carries the message from coast to coast.

All, under God, because one man, left in Lagos, refused to abandon his call.

Lands of the Raj

3
All My Friends Are But One

William Carey 1761–1834

Outside a tumbledown shed on the edge of a steamy swamp a few miles north of Calcutta sat a dejected Englishman. His name was William Carey. The year was 1794. He was thirty-two years old.

In the shed lay his eldest son, desperately ill of dysentery. Beside the boy lay his mother, not only ill but wandering in mind and bitterly reproaching Carey for having dragged them all from a placid English pastorate across dangerous seas to a land of disappointment and destitution. The three other boys (there was a baby too) could not be allowed out of Carey's sight for fear of dacoits – the thieves and brigands who infested the countryside. Although they would disdain to molest a destitute sahib, since fat Indian moneylenders were easy to find, they could get a good price for a kidnapped white child in native states up-country.

The Careys had been in India less than two months and everything had gone wrong. As Carey wiped the sweat off his spectacles, picked up his Bible and turned pages already spoiled by mildew, he wondered whether he had mistaken God's call.

It had all begun more than ten years earlier. Carey,

then twenty-one and a mere village shoemaker in
the Midlands of England, a man of no account in
an aristocratic age but already a fervent Christian,
had been reading a borrowed copy of *Captain Cook's
Voyages*, an especially topical book because the news
of the great explorer's murder by South Sea islanders
had only recently reached Europe. Captain Cook was
not particularly known as a Christian, yet the book
brought the young shoemaker Christ's orders to serve
as His missionary in the South Seas, where none had
so much as heard His name.

Missionaries in the 1780s were an almost extinct
race. When Carey attempted to enthuse his fellow
Baptists with the project, he was rebuffed with the
crushing retort: "When God pleases to convert the
heathen, He'll do it without consulting you!" Carey
became a full-time pastor, and still the Christless
millions overseas dominated his prayers, and even
turned him into a pamphlet writer.

In 1792 he persuaded his brethren to found the
Baptist Missionary Society. They began collecting
a little money, in the form of pledges thrust into a
snuffbox, and designated Carey their first missionary,
to sail to Tahiti as soon as their funds allowed.

"Expect great things from God. Attempt great
things for God", Carey had proclaimed. And here
he was, little more than a year later, sitting on the
edge of an Indian marsh, almost a castaway.

His plan to evangelize the South Seas had been
changed through the influence of a surgeon on leave
from the British East India Company in Bengal.
John Thomas painted a vivid picture of the Hindu
civilization of India. His soul was eaten up by compas-

sion for Indian sufferings, and zeal for the conversion of Indians to Christ, and he believed the time was ripe.

Carey agreed to go to India, with the Baptist missionary committee's approval, but at the cost of separation from his timid, stay-at-home wife until the mission should be established.

Carey, his eldest son Felix, and John Thomas set sail in 1793, only to be put ashore again. The East India Company was implacably opposed to missions, which might endanger commercial profits by angering the Hindus. A friendly captain had smuggled the three aboard. But creditors pursued Thomas who, though a sincere missionary, was totally irresponsible regarding money.

"All I can say," wrote Carey, watching the sails of the convoy of East Indiamen disappear over the horizon, "is that however mysterious the leadings of Providence, I have no doubt but that they are superintended by an infinitely wise God."

Ten days later, his lips filled with praise, Carey was embarking on a Danish ship whose crew cared nothing for the anti-missionary growls of the British company. What is more, Thomas had not only squared his London creditors but Dorothy Carey had rejoined her husband with their whole family, including the new baby.

When the ship reached the mouth of the Ganges, Thomas insisted that they all disembark secretly downstream from Calcutta, partly for fear of more creditors, partly to avoid arrest and expulsion by British officials.

Within two months William Carey, despite the

thrill at his first steps in Bengali, of hearing Thomas
preach in the crowded Bengal villages, and of all the
sights and sounds of India, was on the edge of despair.
The sheer weight of Hinduism seemed to crush hopes
that a Christian church would arise quickly. Dorothy
and Felix fell ill, and Dorothy's mind began to
unhinge. Then John Thomas announced that he
had misjudged their finances and they were nearly
destitute. Carey was reduced to accepting the loan
of a native moneylender's garden house in a neighbourhood abounding in snakes, tigers, and cut-throat
dacoits.

As Carey sat in the steamy heat outside that
shed, his wife moaning in the shadows behind, it
would have been hard to believe that here was the
"father of modern missions" whose translations of the
Scriptures would pioneer missionary work in India,
whose name, when he died, would be known and
honoured from Cape Cormorin to the Himalayas.

The would-be missionary to India might have cut
his losses at that moment. The spirit within him was
too hot to abandon the ministry – he had heard the
call and must follow. But he might have concluded
that the door to India was closing, that he had
mistaken God's guidance when he had agreed to go
to India, and that he had best change back to Tahiti
where there was no entrenched Hinduism, where
no "Christian" company officials would frustrate his
designs.

Carey decided to seek advice from David Brown,
a well-known evangelical chaplain to the East India
Company's Europeans in Calcutta. He walked
through the heat of the city to see Brown, but

Brown received him frigidly because of distrust of John Thomas. In later years Brown and Carey would be close friends, but on this January day of 1794 the chaplain sent his ex-cobbler away without even offering him refreshment after his long walk.

"All my friends are but One," thought Carey as he trudged home again, "but He is all sufficient." In his diary he wrote: "Towards evening felt the all-sufficiency of God, and the stability of His promises, which much relieved my mind. As I walked home in the night, was enabled to roll all my cares on Him."

Soon he was allowed to occupy and clear a small area of jungle in another, more healthy district. He intended to support his family by small farming, like the Indians around him, while learning the language and beginning to preach. Then Thomas secured for him the post of manager of an indigo plantation at Malda several hundred miles away, and the whole situation was transformed.

Carey became a well-paid planter with a pleasant home and unrivaled opportunity for getting to know the language, the people, and their customs as he travelled far and wide, buying the indigo crop and supervising the processes which turned it into the blue vegetable dye much prized in eighteenth-century Europe. In slack periods he could preach and teach. He had a friendly employer, George Udny, a vigorous Christian who as a magistrate could protect Carey from government attempts to forbid his preaching.

The road ahead was not easy. Carey survived a serious attack of malaria, but his little boy Peter did not. Mrs Carey fell ill again and began to rail against her husband. For weeks he endured her violence

against himself and all he held dear, and because
so little was then known about the influence of body
upon mind, it was a long time before he realized that
her ravings and bitterness were part of her illness. To
Carey it seemed that his much-loved Dorothy had
become his enemy.

In the midst of these troubles he received a letter
from the mission committee in England deploring his
being a planter. Had he not, they asked, left England
to be a missionary?

A missionary he was. William Carey, planter of
Malda in Bengal in the closing years of the eighteenth
century, is a sort of patron saint of the many hundreds
of men and women today who are not listed as
"missionaries", yet are full-time missionaries at heart.
They may be in commerce or industry, United Nations or diplomatic service, or in any of the hundred
and one positions open to Western Christians in
lands where Christianity is a minority religion, but
their vocation and intention is to be witnesses and
ambassadors for Christ.

Whereas Carey's employer, George Udny, a devout evangelical, put his secular concerns first (he
loved the Bible and encouraged missionaries but
never preached to Indians himself), Carey put business concerns last. He lived simply and devoted
the bulk of his income to the translation of the
Scriptures. "I am indeed poor, and always shall be,"
he told the home committee, "until the Bible is
published in Bengali and Hindustani and the people
need no further instruction." His considerable spare
time went to translating, or to preaching under the
tamarind tree of each teeming village of the district.

The preaching made no impact on the entrenched hold of Hinduism. All around were the miseries imposed by the caste system, yet its iron grip held the hearts of the people to idolatry. As John Thomas, managing a nearby plantation, wrote to the home committee: "Do not send men of compassion here, for you will break their hearts. Do send men *full* of compassion, for many perish with cold, many for lack of bread, and millions for lack of knowledge."

All but two of Carey's handful of converts proved to be frauds or became backsliders. "I am almost grown callous," he wrote in 1799, "and tempted to preach as if their hearts were invulnerable. But this dishonours the grace and power of God." Meanwhile, he and Thomas had completed the translation of the New Testament into Bengali, and Udny had bought them a printing press.

The future again grew obscure. Several bad seasons and a calamitous flood followed by drought and epidemics made Udny determined to abandon his plantations. Carey would be without a home or a job, and four English missionaries with their families were on the outward voyage to join him. He therefore invested all his savings in buying an indigo plantation to form their base.

One of the new missionaries, William Ward, fresh from landing, reached him with the news that they had been offered land and sanctuary. In the tiny Danish enclave of Serampore, British orders of expulsion could not affect them. And Serampore, only fourteen miles upriver from Calcutta, was a strategic centre, whereas Malda lay remote.

"Carey has made up his mind to leave all and follow

our Saviour to Serampore", wrote Ward. "Indeed, whilst He has opened a door there to us, He has shut all others."

Ward was a printer, his ambition "to *print* among the Gentiles the unsearchable riches of Christ". The other leader of the party, Joshua Marshman, was a self-taught schoolmaster, brilliant but cross-grained, with a wife of inexhaustible good humour. Carey joined them, and for over thirty years the Serampore trio of Carey, Marshman and Ward was the spearhead of Christian work in India.

How Carey translated the whole Bible into five Indian languages, and parts of it into nearly thirty more; how Ward printed the versions and, as converts came, spread them the length and breadth of India; how the Marshmans founded schools to support the community, and Carey taught in the East India Company's college in Calcutta; and how they launched the first mission to Burma which Judson was to join at their suggestion – all this is part of the imperishable saga of the growth of the Church of God.

Yet it would have come to naught had the destitute Carey of January 1794 abandoned his Indian designs and attempted to reach Tahiti. The discouraged recruit became the foremost missionary of his day.

4
Judson's Darkest Hour

Adoniram Judson 1788–1850

The American couple sat down to their meal nervously.

On this June day of 1824 in the Burmese capital of Ava, four hundred miles from the sea, Adoniram and Ann Judson, both in their thirties, lived by sufferance of the Burmese king in a little house he had allowed them to build. The home was of teak, which could not keep out the heat of the day, but it was within sight and sound of the royal palace.

The king was contemptuous of their message as Christian missionaries, and suspicious of their motive. But richly dressed nobles and even the king himself would condescend to listen to their words occasionally when they visited the royal audience rooms. Yellow-robed Buddhist monks filed past their rough veranda, begging bowls in hand, on the way to the bazaar. Sometimes a priest accepted an invitation to listen to the American teacher's earnest declaration that the Truth could be *known*, and that the Way was not a path of merit leading to ultimate Nothingness but a living Person who brought Life.

For twelve years the Judsons had struggled, first in Rangoon, and for the past six months at Ava, the

capital. Their work had at last begun to show the
small beginnings of a Christian church in a Buddhist
land. Now all was at hazard again because war had
broken out between the Burmese and the British,
who had sent an invasion force from India.

The three or four British residents of Ava had
already been thrown into prison. This is why the
Judsons were nervous as they toyed with their food.
The Burmese knew no distinction between the sub-
jects of King George IV and the fellow citizens of
President James Monroe.

The Judson dinner had barely begun when a
Burmese officer rushed in, accompanied by a knot
of men. They were led by a brute whose spotted
face and depraved features proclaimed him a jailer
– a murderer reprieved on condition that he torture
and kill as required.

Despite Ann's protests and her hurried offers of
money, Adoniram Judson was thrown to the ground.
A cord was deftly wound round his upper arms and
chest and tightened until it cut. Then they hurried
him away. When Ann sent their Burmese assistant, a
convert and true friend, to follow the party and again
offer money, the words were barely out of his mouth
before the jailer tripped Judson on the pathway and
tightened the cords until he could barely breathe.

At the jail he was stripped of most of his clothes,
manacled, and placed alongside the other white
captives already in the death prison. The tiny com-
partment was packed with local criminals and crawl-
ing with vermin. He was soon joined by his sole
American missionary colleague, the bachelor Dr
Price.

June heat and the small size of the windows made misery enough. But at night time an atrocious contraption, a long bamboo pole attached to a pulley, was thrust between the fettered legs of each prisoner and jacked up until the weight of his body and the irons had to rest, all night long, on his shoulders and hands.

In the months that followed, Judson survived only through Ann's indomitable courage. Though expecting a baby she daily spent weary hours walking through Ava to petition officials and nobles. She brought him his only food. She smuggled in his New Testament, and she kept up his courage by brief visits, made at the risk of being arrested herself and sent into slavery.

Years earlier, on his first voyage from America Judson had been imprisoned in the hold of an English ship after its capture by a French privateer. He had been tempted then to regret his refusal of the assistant minister's post at the largest church in Boston in preference for the hazards of missionary life.

Such temptation had long lost its force. At Ava he was proving in appalling conditions the accuracy of some gallant words which he had penned in a comfortable New England home when facing the prospect of being the first American preacher in Asia. "O the pleasure which a lively Christian must enjoy in communion with God!" Judson had written. "It is all one whether he is in a city or a desert, among relations or among savage foes, in the heat of the Indies or in the ice of Greenland; his infinite Friend is always at hand. He need not fear want or

sickness or pain, for his best Friend does all things
well. He need not fear death, though it come in the
most shocking form, for death is only a withdrawing
of the veil which conceals his dearest Friend."

In those first days in the death house, as his
cramped limbs, chilled with loss of circulation, were
lowered to the ground in the morning, Judson knew
that his dearest Friend was beside him. When the
bell began tolling the afternoon hour at which victims
would be let out to be beaten or mutilated or
crucified, and a ghastly stillness settled on criminals
and prisoners of war alike, waiting to know who
should be chosen next, Judson proved the peace that
passes understanding.

Days lengthened into months. Conditions became
slightly better, thanks to Ann's persistence, but
a tide of frustration began to mount in Judson's
mind.

His beloved converts were scattered. He could no
longer go out under the shadow of a golden pagoda
to engage passers-by in religious conversation. He
could do no work on the Burmese dictionary which
would enable American reinforcements to learn
the language. Nor could he continue the Burmese
translation of the Bible which he knew was an
essential preliminary to the growth of a strong
church.

What was worse, his imprisonment, unlike the
Apostle Paul's, did not seem to be furthering the
Gospel. It was a mere accident of war. It meant little
to anyone in Ava.

Had Judson been called upon to suffer publicly for
his faith, or to withstand attempted brainwashing like

Geoffrey Bull in China a century and a quarter later, or even to perform hard manual labour in slavery, he could have borne it. To be condemned to lie everlastingly doing nothing in a fetid jail day after day made him depressed and irritable. His faith remained, but his joy was gone.

It returned when the white prisoners were flung back into the inner prison. Their feet were again made fast in the stocks, like Paul's and Silas's at Philippi, and a rumour was strong that they were to be executed at three in the morning. As the hour approached Judson grew calm. When he led the others in prayer his joy at the prospect of the immediate presence of Christ was muted only by sorrow for his wife.

The rumour was false. Then came a period of fever which prostrated his body and spirits. Again he was saved by his wife's intercession. He was allowed to move into a little bamboo hut – until an awful day when the weakened Judson and the others were taken away.

They were to be burned alive as a sacrifice to the spirits who should then give the Burmese victory over the English. No announcement was made, however, of their intended fate.

Judson's fetters were removed, together with the shoes and socks with which Ann had kept her husband supplied. The men were roped together two by two and driven like animals down the sandy, flinty road which was baking in the midday sun. On feet which for nearly a year had been allowed no exercise but a brief fettered hobble round the yard, and which were now unwontedly bare, blisters grew fast and soon burst. Every step was a torture, and the jailers moved their prisoners fast.

Judson's morale collapsed. As they passed high over a watercourse he contemplated throwing himself and his companion to death. "The parapet is low", he gasped. "There can be no sin in our availing ourselves of the opportunity."

A modern biographer of Judson doubts this story, which he had read in the reminiscences of a fellow prisoner writing thirty years after the event. He considers it "difficult to conceive" that even in temporary desperation such a man as Judson could have contemplated both the sin of suicide and the treachery of leaving his wife alone in a hostile land. But Ann Judson confirms the story herself as it was told to her the next day by her husband: "So great was his agony, he ardently longed to throw himself into the water to be free from misery. But the sin attached to such an act alone prevented."

The Lord's words, "I will keep thee in all thy ways", proved true even when Judson was physically past controlling himself. His Lord was at his side; He was intervening in other ways too. The Bengali servant of one of the prisoners caught up with the column and saw their distress. He pulled off his turban, tore it in two and handed half to his master and half to Judson, who tied it around his feet. The servant supported and half-carried Judson the rest of the way.

The prisoners were by now in such poor shape that the eight-mile journey planned by their jailers had to be broken by a night's rest. A kindhearted Burmese woman risked official wrath to refresh them with fruit. But next day, when they had reached the ruined bamboo dwelling which was to be set on fire as soon as they were chained to stakes inside, the situation had changed.

The high government leader who had plotted their execution had fallen from favour and been summarily executed.

Judson's darkest hour passed. The place of intended immolation became a prison where captivity was less rigorous than at Ava. But Ann, who had followed him into the countryside with their baby daughter, fell seriously ill.

Judson was able, however, to look forward with hope, for the British forces advanced slowly up the Irrawaddy. "Here I have been for ten years preaching the Gospel", he remarked to a fellow prisoner, "to timid listeners who wish to embrace the truth but dare not – beseeching the emperor to grant liberty of conscience to his people, but without success. And now, when all human means seem at an end, God opens the way by leading a Christian nation to subdue the country. It is possible that my life will be spared. If so, with what ardour and gratitude shall I pursue my work. And if not, His will be done: the door will be opened for others who will do the work better."

His life was spared. The door was opened, and in a way he could not have foreseen. The Burmese territory newly annexed by the British (who permitted missionary work unreservedly) contained a race, the Karens, of whom Judson had known nothing at the time of his imprisonment. The Karens were mostly animist, not Buddhist, and listened to the Gospel with open ears. The Karen church became

the principal base and spearhead of Christianity
throughout Burma.

Adoniram Judson bore marks of the iron fetters
for the rest of his life. The long imprisonment had
marked him in another way too. He could not bear
to be idle.

When the American mission grew large, and missionaries developed a tendency to concentrate in the
larger centres, Judson pushed out into the wilds. He
travelled endlessly among the Karens and Burmese
whenever his health permitted. He grudged the time
which administrative duties, and even the translation
work and scholarship which he loved, forced him to
spend at his base.

Wherever he went he preached and baptized. He
was in a hurry, as if seeking to recover the years
lost in prison. Judson would not wait until a convert
had grown old and wise. When any man he met on
tour sought baptism, having heard the Gospel from
a native evangelist, Judson would question him and
his neighbours closely. He believed that if the man
had been born again the fact would be evident in his
transformed life and baptism need not be delayed.
Judson was seldom deceived, and the Karen church
grew fast.

Before the prison years, evangelization had de-
pended almost entirely on his own labours. When
Judson's feet were bound in the stocks, the Word
of God had seemed shackled. He sought therefore
to extend himself by urging his converts to go out two
by two through the jungle paths to distant villages.
He was among the first missionaries to teach that
a church must be self-propagating. Thus the Karen

church grew and became strong. Its members were outward looking, willing to suffer hardship, danger, and long absences from home to enable others to know Christ as the One who delivers from fear and despair.

Judson's twenty months of stench and frustration in Ava's jails had not been futile after all.

5
He Tamed the Tribes

Sir Herbert Edwardes 1819–1868

Early in 1847 a young British subaltern of Bengal Infantry set out on a task to quell the stoutest. Lieutenant Herbert Edwardes had been ordered from Peshawar, the dust-ridden frontier town of the Punjab at the foot of the wild Khyber Pass, to bring peace and government to the Bannu Valley.

Bannu was a paradise of nature, but its people were lawless, "robbers and murderers from their cradles". They butchered one another and had refused to pay taxes to their overlords, the Sikhs, whom the British had lately conquered. As Edwardes said, they "wear arms as we wear clothes, and use them as we use knives and forks", while the Sikh soldiers with him would be looking for nothing but loot.

Edwardes, a vivacious young man with laughing eyes, who could as easily turn from soldiering to writing essays and verses, and who had a remarkable capacity for friendship, was not afraid. He had fought in the recent war with distinction, but courage of a different kind was needed now. His fearlessness sprang from his faith. He believed that it was God who was sending him to heal a tortured land. And he knew that his Saviour was beside him as the column toiled upwards, beneath forbidding rocks and over turbulent streams, with the hot Indian sun above.

When Edwardes reached the Valley, some of the Bannus fled to the hills, others stayed in sullen fear. Soon they were astonished by this lone Englishman whose strange power belied his youthful face. They saw looting suppressed by instant punishment. When, suspicious and diffident, they brought complaints and arguments, Edwardes heard them with patience, good humour, and kindness. When they tried to deceive him, he knew it instinctively and would punish them as he punished the Sikhs. Warring chiefs were soon sitting together beside him; four hundred forts were destroyed at his word; even the taxes were paid. "In my little sphere," he wrote, "I gave my whole soul for the establishment of that vast and priceless blessing, peace." And early each morning, in the quiet of his tent, Edwardes would lay all his problems, dangers, and hopes before his Lord.

The pacification of Bannu was the first of many achievements which brought Edwardes resounding fame – crushing rebellion at Multan, bringing peace and prosperity to the intractable tribes of Jalandhar, and negotiating in the face of official opposition and disbelief a treaty of alliance with the powerful Amir of Afghanistan. But good administration was not enough. Edwardes' greatest desire was to see the fanatical Muslims of the hills and the Hindus and Sikhs of the plains united at the foot of the Cross. As agent of the government he was forbidden to preach, but when a fellow officer, Colonel Martin, approached him as Commissioner of Peshawar for

leave to found a mission, Edwardes gave wholehearted support, and in 1855 was able to introduce
the first two missionaries of the Border Mission and
see the first native Christian baptized.

Edwardes was one of that remarkable band of
unashamed Christians who transformed the tyran-
nized, blood-drenched Sikh kingdom into the pros-
perous and contented British Punjab. The gay Henry
Lawrence, "father" and master of them all, who was
killed in the siege of Lucknow; his wife Honoria, who
rode with them, worked, prayed, and endured with
them; his brother John, afterwards Viceroy, dour and
severe but earnest in his faith; young Nicholson, who
died a hero's death at Delhi – the basis of their life
was faith in Christ. "This morning he read a chapter
of the Bible to George and me," wrote Edwardes of
Henry Lawrence at Lucknow during a visit a bare
month before the Mutiny, "and then he prayed with
great earnestness . . . The whole prayer was for
peace and forbearance and good-will and the help
of Christ Himself in our whole lives."

By their Christian characters such administrators
did much to prove to Eastern races the love and
power of Christ. They would have done more. "The
greatest and oldest and saddest of India's wants",
said Edwardes, "is religious truth, a revelation of
the real nature of the God whom for ages she
has been ignorantly worshipping." Edwardes and
his friends recognized that the government itself
could not attempt to convert, but they believed
the accepted policy of absolute religious neutrality
to be harmful. Had the Bible been taught in the
native schools, false views of Christianity would

not have spread, the Mutiny might never have occurred, and India would steadily have yielded to Christ. "An open Bible," pleaded Edwardes, "put it in your schools, stand avowedly as a Christian government." Only then would India be truly fitted for freedom, "leavened with Christianity".

When the storm came in 1857, the Punjab stood firm. The Afghans abided by Edwardes' treaty and took no advantage of British troubles. At Peshawar Edwardes and Nicholson boldly disarmed the mutinous regiments. "If Peshawar goes," a loyal Sikh sirdar had said, "the whole Punjab will be rolled up in rebellion." And had the Punjab revolted, all Bengal might have fallen.

Yet it is not the statesmanship of Sir Herbert Edwardes that is relevant today so much as his witness to a layman's influence for Christ in the ordinary course of his calling. "I never knew anyone so bold in confessing Christ as Edwardes was", said a brother officer on the Frontier. "Many of us felt as he did but we had not the courage to avow it." "This great country India," Edwardes would say, "has been put into our hands that we may give it light." Edwardes' words are still a challenge: "Other dependent races in other parts of the world are equally in heathen darkness. If we are looking for the coming of our Lord again upon the earth, we surely should bestir ourselves to gather in as much of His inheritance as we can while time is left."

Edwardes was barely forty-nine when he died, on sick leave in Scotland in 1869. "Jesus only . . . Triumphant Jesus", were his last words. "I am quite happy. I trust entirely to Jesus and I couldn't do more if I lived a thousand years!"

The news was telegraphed to India and carried into the hills. An old, bent Muslim heard it and found his way to a missionary. "I lived with Sir Herbert all the years he has been in India," said the old servant, "and I followed him everywhere. My sahib was *such* a good man. He can't have made a mistake in his religion. Will you teach me his religion? for I should like to believe what he believed."

6
The Lame Cow's Friend

Rosalie Harvey 1854–1932

On 26th March 1884, a dark-haired, frail looking young English woman stepped from the Down-Mail at Nasik Road station, a pet dog in her arms. Rosalie Harvey was one of the numerous children of the Vicar of Seaford in Sussex. She had offered for missionary work in 1874 at twenty, but the doctors were sceptical and not until 1882 did she reach India. Her father thought she would stand three years. She stayed fifty, with one brief break.

After two years in Poona she came to Nasik. And for the first time drove in a *tonga* along the road from the railway, under massive banyan trees, roots draping from their branches, and the clumps of golden mohurs, their flowers bright red in the sun, to the Mission compound, former summer palace of the Mahratta Peishwas, but now "with no shadow of the claim to the title of palace". Yet the inner hall, separated from the verandas by cane screens on which flickered the light of a lamp suspended from the high ceiling, "rivalled in quaintness anything I had yet seen".

Nasik, the sacred city of Western India, close to the source of the sacred Godavari, which flows across the

Deccan down to the Bay of Bengal, had a fine climate
and natural beauty, offset by the bigotry of its priests
and Brahmins; even the railway, which at Benares
runs in sight of the bathing *ghats*, had been kept six
miles off.

Rosalie's mission worked among women, who by
both Hindu and Muslim custom were segregated in
zenanas.[1] Her gay spirit was undeterred by difficulties, and she was soon immersed in the normal work
of a zenana missionary.

A girls' school had been started – in a haunted
house, the only one extracted from reluctant land-
lords – and Rosalie and her colleague opened others,
to which small boys also were admitted. She visited
zenanas, and the jail. She wished she could open a
pauper widows' home: "how many poor old people
are left to die of neglect and distress just because they
are old and useless. If someone would leave me a
fortune how gladly I would open such a Refuge!" She
began a school for high-caste married girls, for *purdah*
was not much observed among Hindus in Western
India and they could go to and from their zenanas
with little restraint. "Think what the result would be",
she wrote, "if a hundred Brahmin girls of Nasik, wives
in name but children in reality, were brought daily
into contact with the influence of Christian ladies,
whose sole aim would be to promote their temporal
and spiritual welfare."

She visited in the villages, where the Gospel was
more readily accepted than in the proud homes of

[1]The Zenana Bible and Medical Mission became later the Bible
and Medical Missionary Fellowship, working among both sexes,
and is now Interserve, operating in several countries.

the city, and whenever she found a girl or a child-wife suffering, the offending males would be astonished at the vigour with which this shy and retiring Miss Sahib would berate them with her tongue. "You dare to admit it to me openly?" she retorted to a husband whose maltreatment of his childwife had caused injury to her spine. "Get out of this room at once!"

"Will this city ever become Christian?", she wrote one evening, after walking back through the dimly lit streets and glancing in at the dark interiors where vegetable-oil lamps feebly flickered. "The people seem so to be locked up in Hinduism, so content – so hopelessly content to let things go on as they have ever gone."

Early in January 1887 Rosalie was walking to her latest school. "On the way, met a drove of cattle and a woman beating a cow whose leg was broken. I stopped her, and took the cow away and took it to our bungalow. . . . This is only one of the many instances which one comes across in this country of lame or maimed cattle being driven into the jungle when they ought to be at home."

Rosalie knew well that a Hindu would never kill a cow, since it is sacred, but cheerfully leave it to die in agony, and could be callous to animals and work them to death.

She decided then and there that this had gone on long enough. In the absence of the Collector (the principal civil officer), the Civil Surgeon was the leading English resident. "So I thought, 'I will go at once to him while the feeling is hot upon me', and off I started. It was nearly ten o'clock, and the sun was getting hot, but I could not stop to get a *tonga*, and to bring one from the town would take so long. Taking the gardener with me, I started across the plain and arrived at the doctor's bungalow with a red, hot face, my sun topi turned down, and I fear, a slightly crazy appearance, but all this would help to make an impression. . . .

"Before I got to the door the doctor was out on the veranda to see who was come, flying in with a native flying after. He said, 'This is an unexpected pleasure.' I replied, 'Please don't think I'm mad – don't think I'm mad!' and then related the circumstances. As I did so, the recollection of the poor animal's pain made the tears come into my eyes, and I could scarcely speak for crying. The doctor said, 'We can do nothing. There is no Royal Humane Society here.' Then I said, 'Can't we get one?' He did not seem to think that it was either practicable or possible, and I felt chafed at this restraint. 'We ought, we English ought to do something', I said. 'We ought not to stand by and see these things go on.'"

The lame cow became a permanent inmate of the mission compound. In September it was joined by an ox, whom Rosalie had found yoked to a heavy quarry cart, despite a gaping wound in its neck; she sent for the Deputy Collector, "who was disgusted at the men's cruelty".

A month later a donkey came, a large wound in its chest and side. The donkey's owner asked for it back. "I told the young man that he could stop in the compound day and night if he liked and see that his animal was safe, but that if he took it away now I should summons him for cruelty. The watchman told the people about the cow and the ox that have been rescued, and after loitering about a bit they went away." A little later "a man came here with a cow with a broken leg for me to mend. Was obliged to tell him this is not a 'Cow Hospital', tho' I wish it were." The next day "Donkey's owner came bothering about the donkey; got into a rage with him; at which he was somewhat subdued. He says, 'I am a poor man – give me back my donkey!' I say, 'You are a poor man, therefore I will feed and doctor your donkey for you, and when it is well I will give it back to you.' He says again, 'I am a poor man, give me back my donkey. I will give it better food than you do.' Then I turned on him and told him to '*chup* and go'. He wants to make me buy it."

Before the end of 1887 Rosalie had badgered the local Indian and English notables to found a branch of the Bombay Society for the Prevention of Cruelty to Animals, which took financial responsibility for the growing array of maimed, tired and diseased cattle in the compound yard, and built "a kind of hospital", a collection of sheds close by.

For two years Rosalie bore the brunt of the Animal Hospital management in addition to her other work, until a veterinary officer was appointed. From her scanty personal allowance she was already supporting two three-legged calves, Sonya and Bapu, old Tommy the horse, and the big buffalo Ahjiba, to say nothing of two human babies. As Rosalie wrote in her diary, "It *is* difficult to work things properly in Nasik. . . . There is money – money for bribes – money for unjust stewards who keep back money meant for Government purposes – money for useless feasts and vices – but for the poor and needy how hard it is to get money – like drawing a heavy bucket from a deep well!

"If they won't give of their abundance – oh, that God would entrust some of that abundance to me, and with it wisdom to dispense it wisely! . . . I long to build a new Hospital for Animals, schools for the Mission and a new Z.M. House, with such rooms for the agents and servants, as we now also much feel the need of. Lord Jesus, hear my prayer. Indulge my long-cherished and ardent wish."

In 1892 she paid a visit to the famous Animal Hospital near Bombay. On the drive back to the city her companion, Mr Hills, promised to try to get money from old Sir Dinshaw Petit, a Parsi millionaire baronet and cotton millowner, the real founder of Bombay's industrial power and a great philanthropist.

Reports were sent, including photographs of Sonya and Bapu hopping on their three legs, and a note describing the amputations. On 1st November Rosalie was taken by a mutual Parsi friend to Sir Dinshaw's magnificent house on Malabar Hill, close to the sea. As they entered the large hall, "out of a side room an old gentleman came, wearing a cashmere dressing gown and a cap on his head. He was a nice looking man. . . . In shaking hands I bowed to him. He looked a little surprised and then returned the bow." He promised Rs. 5,000 provided the hospital was called after him, and to endow it later. As Rosalie discovered, "it was the calves with three legs that did it".

Lord Harris, Governor of Bombay, laid the foundation stone of the Sir Dinshaw Petit Hospital for Animals in January 1895.

To Rosalie's delight, one of her dogs, Tippoo

Sultan, went and "sat under the Governor's chair before he came. When I pointed this out to the Secretary with an air of great satisfaction he said solemnly, 'I think he had better be removed'. Darling Tippoo! He was there to receive the Governor on behalf of all the animal world – and he was to 'be removed' – led off on his chain!"

Rosalie's dogs were one of the features of missionary life at Nasik. "They were by no means always of high degree", wrote a colleague; "if some were handsome some were the reverse." Butterfly was a prince, but even Rosalie admitted that Spot was a "cross between a Pig and a Bear". Sometimes they fought, or bit the Collector's dog. One October there was desolation when Rosalie's favourite, Piggy, disappeared. All Nasik was set looking for him, from the magistrate to schoolchildren. "No news of Piggy", Rosalie wrote in her diary on 14th October. "Does 'if any of thine be driven out unto the utmost part of heaven' refer to dogs? If it does, then there is hope in the promise, 'From thence will I bring them back'. . . ." "Piggy! Piggy!", she wrote three days later, "all day long I am thinking of him. Will he come back again?" On the evening of 1st November some small boys said they had found Piggy. "Ran with the small boys and Bhaskar Rao to the Chandolkar's Ali – but the dog tied up there was a dog like Tippoo. It was not Piggy. Rao sahib's *tonga* came racing to meet us, and all the household was in expectation – and all faces fell when I said, 'It is not he'. . . . Piggy! Piggy!" He never came back.

During the closing years of the nineteenth century
and the first of the twentieth India experienced a
succession of famines and plagues. In Nasik these
terrible years not only gave Rosalie more work than
she had ever had, but brought forward two causes
close to her heart – the cause of the lepers, and the
cause of the babies.

Lepers had long come for alms to the Mission
bungalow. "Those who are not too lame", wrote
Rosalie in May 1893, "crawl to our bungalow on
Sunday to receive alms and to listen to the service,
which I really think they enjoy."

The lepers of Nasik, about thirty in number,
"haunted the river-side by day and slept on the
verandas of the temples at night, their chief haunt
being the Bell Temple called also Naro Shankar's
temple. The front of this sacred place is rented by
sweetmeat sellers, and in front of these shops the
lepers used to sit exposing their sores, and black
with flies. People shuddered as they passed them,
and one day a man stopped me as I was crossing
the river and exclaimed, 'You have built a hospital
for animals. Why can't you build a home for these
poor people?'"

"Asked the lepers if we should build them an
asylum", Rosalie wrote in December 1893. "They
said, 'Oh do, Sahib – but let it be in the temple
neighbourhood, and make provision for our food'."
It was obvious that mere shelter was not enough, yet
there was no money to build a fully equipped asylum.
A few weeks later, "a poor cripple leper cried out to
me, 'Sahib, I cannot walk, I cannot come to your
bungalow now.' I saw that he couldn't, poor fellow.

Near the lepers' refuge there is a tree where we might go on Sundays and preach to them and give them alms." This they did, especially as the contemporary medical view of leprosy frowned on encouraging them to come through the city to reach the Mission House, now moved from the Peishwa's palace to a better site.

Early in 1897 Rosalie was asked by the Collector to join the Famine Relief Committee. The monsoon had failed and distress was grievous, but funds were pouring into India from Britain and abroad, and relief work – railway and road building, bridging and quarrying – for the able bodied, and Free Kitchens for the weak were organized by the Government. Every day Rosalie and her colleagues were at the kitchens helping the Collector and his committee or distributing blankets and grain, rescuing the helpless and weeding out able-bodied shirkers. She did not forget the lepers. "Went down to tell the lepers they would get food from the kitchen. . . . The poor lepers were very grateful."

The monsoon, late, broke the famine. Then came bubonic plague, from China or, as some said, brought by pilgrims from Mecca, sweeping up-country along the railway lines. In October the administration ordered evacuation of the plague-infected parts of the city, threatening to send in British troops to clear out those who remained. "*18th October, 1897*. Monday . . . We are closing one school after the other. . . . Wherever one went, one met people going out of Nasik with their bundles on their heads. They all wore a look of great amusement. No one seemed to mind." To the lepers, the evacuation was disaster. "When the people were gone," wrote Rosalie, "who was there of whom the lepers could beg? Not only were they starving but their miserable shelter also was gone. They with the rest of the people had to leave the city, and had literally no place to flee into. The nights were bitterly cold, they had very little bedding and they lay shivering on the hillside in the vicinity of Indra Kund. Here there had been created a small plague shed, but it had caught fire and all that remained to shelter the lepers from the cold night winds were the bare posts and rafters blackened by smoke. In this miserable apology for a shelter I found them awaiting death." At Rosalie's behest the Collector supplied sacking, and a daily dole of flour, dal and rice.

Her days were now spent in the Plague Hospital and Segregation Camps, nursing, changing clothes and bedding, cheering the friendless and comforting the dying. The Mission House was compulsorily evacuated after dead rats – the worst plague-carriers – had been found. Rosalie lived in a tent at the hospital, and then at the Church Missionary Society (C.M.S.) bungalow nearby.

To the lepers, thanks to Rosalie, instead of starvation the plague had brought food and shelter. "They look so well," she wrote, "having been fed regularly for six months. They beg us to continue the dole – always. If the Mission could only build and endow an Asylum down near the river, they would all no doubt come into it. How I would love to build one for them! . . ."

When the plague receded the Relief Committee gave notice that the dole would cease and the temporary shelter be taken back. "If I cannot raise money for them," Rosalie wrote, "then they will have to leave their present refuge just as the rains break, and wander about the river banks without food and shelter. They will have to beg, as they did before. No one seems inclined to realize how hard their lot is – and they trust to me to stave off all this that is coming upon them. How to meet so huge a demand I do not know – to feed thirty-two lepers daily, and to build them a home! . . . Poor people! They feel so sure I will do something for them. O good Lord, let them not lack and suffer hunger. Open up a way of escape, as Thou didst for the lepers of old."

The Zenana Mission had no funds to help. The Mission to Lepers was sympathetic but could not offer ready support. The Collector nobly continued official aid for a further month (and gave from his own pocket), and Rosalie went to Bombay to raise money. She wrote to *The Times of India* and called on Sir Dinshaw Petit, "who was very jovial and gave me Rs. 100", which provided a corrugated iron roof. "Even strangers could not withstand an appeal from her," wrote a colleague, "for it would be couched in such racy and clever terms as to be quite irresistible."

Money came slowly, for times were hard. Hindus feared that her proposal to build an asylum was mere cover for proselytizing, while "Christians grumble because so few of the lepers become Christians. . . . The course is to relieve pain unconditionally, and to tell the lepers what we believe to be the remedy for future suffering. Only the Holy Spirit can bring home to their hearts the truths which fall upon their ears." In January 1900 Rosalie made a sketch plan of the proposed asylum, but before sufficient had been raised plague struck again, "like the waves of a hungry sea".

"A postman at the city P.O. says every fifteen minutes a corpse is carried by", she noted in June 1900; the burning ground was "white with the ashes of the newly burned dead." In September, as famine once more stalked the burnt-up land, Government sanctioned the new site for the Leper Asylum.

Rosalie's lepers adored her. "A man of the carpenter caste – not a bad leper – came. I allotted him a place in the shed with the old lepers, whereupon they began to abuse him. As remonstrances did no good I went into the room, gave the ringleader two cuts with my umbrella, kicked their cooking vessels over, and told them to clear out into Naru Shankar's temple." Another time, after a Hindu had made them a present of old sepoy blue coats and red caps, "when I next went to issue the food I found them all lined up in military order, and was greeted with a sepoy salaam. The lamest of the lot said that nothing more was needed but my word of command for them all to go off to chase the dacoit who was terrifying the neighbourhood!"

The lepers called her *Aayi* (Marathi for Mother). "They used to beg for themselves," she said, "but now their 'Mother' begs for them. I have a very helpless family."

The famine of 1900 raised her number from thirty-two to over a hundred. The first permanent building on the asylum site was opened in 1901 – a home for untainted children. The Mission to Lepers had assumed responsibility, with Miss Harvey as superintendent so long as she wished, and the Leper

Asylum at last opened, with wards for men and women, a dispensary and a school room, in 1903. "I am aiming at things beyond my power," she had written ten years before, "but not beyond the power of God."

.   .   .   .   .

When Rosalie was a young missionary, fresh from England, she was taken round the wards of the Civil Hospital. Seeing a mere skeleton of a baby tossing in its cot she asked why it was restless. "The baby does not want a doctor, but a mother", replied the English Civil Surgeon; "you take it home and care for it." Her senior missionary refused permission; when Rosalie told the doctor, he looked her in the face and said, "If missionaries won't do this work, then who will?"

At Nasik in January 1889 the Indian Matron of the maternity hospital asked Rosalie to take a little girl, the child of Brahmin parents. The parents had no use for this baby, Sita, and she would have been left, like so many babies in India at that time, to die in the fields, or to be thrown into a well or a ditch. Rosalie found an *amma* for Sita ("It is not difficult to get a foster mother in India," she wrote, "because so many babies die"), and brought them to live in the mission compound. On 2nd March the baby was baptized but three weeks later she died. "If an adopted child can take such a hold on one, what must it be to own a real child? And when I see her, she will know me and love me as she could not know me and love me here. The empty cot – her clothes are lying about – I can't put them away, her nurse has gone home – sorrowfully relinquishing her place."

Six months later Rosalie adopted another, Venu, a week old. "Venubai's mother wanted to know when I would take her away!", and announced that she would leave the hospital in four days, regardless of the fate of the child. But her callousness had already been fatal, for Venu died in the hospital. In 1890, prison visiting, Rosalie found a young Gujerati girl-widow with a three-months-old baby which she had tried to kill. "She said she had wandered all over Bombay asking people to take it, but no one would. She had not gone to the 'white people'. I told her I would take it." In 1891 a man of good caste who had lost his wife carried their baby girl, dosed with opium, the six miles into Nasik and dumped it at Rosalie's feet. He bluntly informed me that if I did not take it he was to make it over to the dancing-girls. Though a healthy child of about six weeks old, it was reduced to a skeleton."

And so the list grew; a baby Brahmin boy, who grew up be the delight of Rosalie's later years, was adopted in 1894. Rescue work was not easy, for until the famine the "natives would rather see their children die than become Christians".

The famine turned Rosalie's personal adopted family into an official Babies' Home, authorized by the Mission at Christmas 1896, Government undertaking to make a grant for each child. As it happened, though other districts were swamped with orphans, her seven babies were not at first joined by others, even when she put an advertisement in the Press. "It is sad to think," she commented, "that in one locality children are starving to death, in others we have to hunt for them."

Seeing her advertisement a Hindu official asked if conversion was intended. Rosalie replied unequivocally: "My offer as a missionary, to receive girls of three to ten years of age, who through the famine have lost all their natural guardians, necessarily includes the placing of them in a Mission School, where they will be brought up in the Christian religion."

Rosalie at once planned a proper building for the foundlings, and before long they were arriving: "A baby was brought in a basket with a blanket erected over it by means of bent reeds. A man carried the basket on his head, a police sepoy walked by the side with a large official letter, and a coolie followed with a tin pot containing milk. Despite all these arrangements the infant was wailing, and only stopped when it got into its natural element – a mother's arms." In 1900, with the famine at its height, the Babies' Home was opened in the Mission compound.

The babies, often coming in two at a time whenever the missionaries visited the relief camps, would be put in groups with foster mothers, "responsible women who have lost their babies. They live in little rooms in the compound." The babies would grow up not knowing they were orphans. A Parsi convert was chief assistant, and in 1901 Rosalie was joined by a young Englishwoman who was to be with her for the rest of her life and succeed to her work at the Babies' Home.

As the famine and plague receded the Babies' Home remained. "In our Mission," Rosalie wrote in 1902, "we all meet morning and evening for prayers. All the babies come, however small, and sometimes a dog or two. All the heathen servants come. Sometimes the babies crow, and make a joyful noise or walk about the church."

.   .   .   .   .

Rosalie had yet another dream: that Nasik's women should have their own efficient hospital. She even said, "If I were younger I would come home and study medicine myself."

A Hindu widow had founded a hospital for women, but few entered because only a cactus hedge separated it from the men's hospital and no woman surgeon or physician served on the staff. It was about to close.

Rosalie harried its trustees to sell and the Mission to buy and equip and send out a lady doctor. She had no direct responsibility for the medical mission, once the new hospital had opened in 1903, but regarded it as the "crowning happiness" of her life's work.

She refused to return to Europe for a furlough, and took only one holiday in the hills to recover her health after the plague years, until in 1906 she at last agreed to an eleven-month rest in New Zealand, where her brother lived.

She returned to Nasik on the evening of 21st November 1907. Everyone was at the station to meet her. "The old groom was overwhelmed with joy and flinging himself on her neck and kissing her, he cried, 'Oh, Mother! Mother!' while her poor hat was sent rolling in the dust." At the bungalow the children let off fireworks. The lepers held a thanksgiving service and recited poems in her honour. Next day she went once again to the Animals' Home.

She worked on, for another sixteen years, seeing a better hospital built in a healthy suburb, and the Babies' Home run by her devoted assistant.

Her concern for animals never wavered. Pained by the condition of the bullocks who drew the town's water carts, she formed a relief corps to give the regulars occasional rests. She instituted periodic inspections of *tonga* ponies. "Would you", runs a typical letter to the Collector, "be able to attend a meeting of the Nasik S.P.C.A. at the Sir D. M. Petit Animal Hospital some time this month or next? We wish to protest against the condition of the Nasik tram ponies and horses. They are miserably thin now, and as the weather gets hotter and traffic increases their condition will grow worse and worse." Once she was badly bitten by a monkey, and for some months was seriously ill. She refused to have an operation, and when convalescent went about with a chain and weight round the leg to counteract the contraction, with success.

In 1924, on reaching the age of seventy, Rosalie Harvey was officially retired. She went to live at the Lepers' Home, where she continued as Superintendent, occupying the bungalow across the road with its gay bougainvillea and pleasant garden, where with her dogs, books, photographs and memories she remained the human inspiration and the delight of all Christian workers in Nasik.

Every day after her retirement "Aayi" would walk round the Lepers' Home, a loved figure in her deaconess dress and veil, with a shiny stick to lean on, attending service in the chapel (where grain and water were always left in case birds flying about during service should be trapped when the doors were locked), seeing that all the lepers were happy, encouraging those in pain, having a word with the Biblewoman or the blind Christian minstrel, and then passing on to children's home.

In the last months, before her death in 1932, her jubilee year of missionary service, the lepers ruled their Superintendent, but no one could suggest separating Aayi from her family.

China's Millions

7
Young Man with a Pigtail

Hudson Taylor 1832–1905

Old carpenter Wang wandered down the street towards the river, the mighty Yangtze, so broad that the farther shore looked like a mere smudge on the horizon.

All around were the familiar sights and sounds of a small Chinese town of the eighteen-fifties: loose-trousered peasants carrying their baskets on long bamboo poles across their shoulders, vendors shouting their wares, women hobbling on tightly bound little feet; a teacher, in the robe of his class, trod delicately to avoid the offal; scavenger dogs snarled and fought. Wang knew no other world. He had heard of Outer Barbarians beyond the Middle Kingdom, and pitied them that they could never taste civilization, though he had been told that a few of the more adventurous traded with the Celestial Empire.

His eye caught sight of a knot of excited townsfolk, and as he drew near he saw an extraordinary sight – a "foreign devil". No wonder the crowd was amused: the young man had sandy hair and large grey-blue eyes, a most odd combination for a human being. And even odder were his clothes – black trousers like a coolie's only narrower, black coat complete with pleats and buttons back and front reaching to his knees, leather boots. And no pigtail.

The foreign devil answered questions patiently and began to preach . . . about one Jesus who came into the world and died on a cross, like the poor criminals, Wang supposed, whom sometimes you saw suffer the "death of a thousand pieces". Wang caught snatches. But he could not pay close attention. He was absorbed in study of the foreign devil's amazing clothes, and edged closer to get a better view until almost next to the man, who evidently spotted this rapt interest and directed his talk right at him.

The foreigner paused.

Wang spoke up. "Yes, yes", he said. "What you say is doubtless very true. But, honourable Foreign Teacher, may I ask you a question?"

The young foreigner looked delighted.

"Foreign Teacher, I have been pondering all the while you have been preaching. But the subject is no clearer to my mind. The honourable garment you are wearing has upon one edge of it a number of circular objects that might do duty as buttons, and on the opposite edge, certain slits in the material probably intended for buttonholes?"

The Foreign Teacher seemed disappointed. "Yes, that is so", he murmured.

"The purpose of that strange device I can understand", Wang continued. "It must be to attach the honourable garment in cold or windy weather. But, Foreign Teacher, this is what I cannot understand. What can be the meaning of those buttons in *the middle of the honourable back?*"

"Why, yes," chorused Wang's neighbours, "in the

middle of the back!"

The poor deflated preacher (who had no idea why a Victorian frock coat always had three buttons in the small of the back) soon wandered sadly away, for after Wang's question he was quite unable to draw the crowd back to the great subject of the Good News he had risked his life to bring to inland China, where no foreigner might lawfully go.

James Hudson Taylor, the Foreign Teacher as Wang had called him, was only twenty-three. He came from Yorkshire, England, and had been in China two years. He was small and of sickly physique, which today probably would never have passed the doctors. He was impulsive, warm-hearted and merry, though with a streak of introspective melancholy. His consuming passion was to win Chinese to Christ. He felt thoroughly impatient with the little band of missionaries then in China, who clung to the coast attempting to reproduce for the Chinese the church life and church buildings of England and America.

Hudson Taylor had gone inland. Yet his attempts were failing because he was a foreigner. . . . "In the middle of the honourable back" – the words flung themselves at him, summing up the absurdity of wearing Western dress in the China of those days, where everything foreign was utterly despised.

To put on Chinese dress, pigtail and all, would scandalize brother missionaries and infuriate Western merchants, who would consider that he betrayed the British Empire by demeaning himself in the eyes of the natives. Hudson Taylor, however, had already seen what would not be generally accepted by missionaries for another two generations. As he wrote some years later: "Why should a foreign aspect be given to Christianity? We wish to see churches of such believers presided over by pastors and officers of their own countrymen, worshipping God in their own tongue, in edifices of a thoroughly native style."

Such words were revolutionary. Their spirit remains pertinent, for if differences of dress are no longer a wall between Westerners and Orientals, other barriers remain, or are thrown up. Western confidence that we know best still bedevils some missionary situations, and Hudson Taylor points to the way out – the way of identification. And to the cost: when he adopted Chinese dress, pigtail and all, he lost the respect of his Western contemporaries. But he won the love of the Chinese, could travel widely, be heard quietly, free from urchins who jeered "Foreign Devil!" and earnest inquirers who ruined openair sermons by awkward questions about buttons.

Furthermore, Hudson Taylor is proof that youth is no bar to being God's recipient of new insights. He is a lasting example of the lead that young men (or women) may sometimes give the Church of Christ if they are walking close to Him and will let Him grant them imagination, courage, and persistence, even when, like Hudson Taylor, they are obscure in name and background, without wealth or influence or particularly good health.

The long life of Hudson Taylor, founder of the China Inland Mission (now the Overseas Missionary Fellowship) and one of the greatest of all missionaries, teaches many other lessons, such as the Principle of Faith immortalized by his words, "Depend upon it, God's work done in God's way will never lack for supplies." And the realization that the way to get men and means for the mission field is to deepen the churches until, imbued with the Holy Spirit, their priorities come right and they put the spread of the Gospel before the solace of themselves.

Before he could teach such lessons or find his lifework, the opening of all inland China to the Word of God, the young Hudson Taylor had to learn that courage, initiative, and passion for souls are not enough.

In 1856, about a year after the incident of the Buttons-in-the-Honourable-Back, Hudson Taylor in his pigtail, rock-crystal spectacles, and teacher's robe, returned to Shanghai from Swatow,[1] a notoriously wicked tropical port nearly a thousand miles to the south, where with an elderly Scottish missionary he had laboured happily, if haphazardly and without apparent effect, for five months. Unable to secure a preaching hall Taylor, who was a physician though not yet qualified, knew what he would do – sail back up the coast to Shanghai, collect medicines and his surgical instruments, and return to labour on in Swatow.

He reached Shanghai to find the building where he had left his entire stock of medical supplies burned to cinders. Except for a few instruments all was gone. "My disappointment and trial were very great", he wrote. Vexed and puzzled he determined to go

[1]In this book Chinese names are spelt in the traditional way, in use at the time of the incidents and more familiar than the new *pin yin* spelling.

down the network of canals to Ningpo, the next
Treaty Port, where he might buy some replacements
from a missionary friend; afterwards he would sail
to Swatow.

In the intense summer heat he travelled at a
leisurely pace, preaching and distributing tracts,
until the low level of the Grand Canal made further
progress by boat impossible. Taylor set out before
sunrise through a district disturbed by civil strife,
intending to reach a seaport whence he could take
a junk to Ningpo.

Everything went wrong. Leaving his servant (whom
he had only recently engaged) to bring on the baggage
coolies, Taylor hobbled off in his tight Chinese shoes.
At the first stage he had a tedious wait in a tea-shop
before the coolies straggled in exhausted. They were
opium smokers. He dismissed them, and made the
servant engage others, and stupidly walked ahead.

He never saw servant, coolies, or baggage again.
At the second stage he waited hours. "I felt somewhat
annoyed, and but that my feet were blistered and the
afternoon very hot, I should have gone back to meet
them and urge them on." At dusk there was no
sign except a rumour that they had passed through
towards the sea. Taylor spent a miserable flea-ridden
night in the public dormitory of a tumbledown inn,
and awoke feeling sick. Next day he pushed towards
the coast, and though at a half-way house during a
short shower of rain he managed to preach a little,
he reached the seaport upset and unhappy.

Inquiries were fruitless. He was questioned by the
police, who saw that he was a foreigner. At dusk
he was refused by two inns because the police were

shadowing him, and turned out of another which at first had accepted him. Still searching for a bed he was led around, desperately tired and sore, by a young man who pretended to be friendly but deserted him at one in the morning, so that he had to sleep in the open on the rough steps of a temple where he was in danger of murder by three thieves. He kept himself awake by singing hymns and repeating portions of Scripture and praying aloud in English until the ruffians disappeared in disgust. At last he slept.

He was awakened rudely at sunrise by the young man, who demanded payment for his time the previous night. This was the last straw. When the fellow laid hands on him Hudson Taylor lost his temper. He grasped the man's arm and shouted at him to shut up.

Everything, everyone was against Hudson. The baggage containing almost all he possessed had been stolen by his faithless servant. Any hope of getting to Ningpo was lost, and somehow, almost penniless, entirely friendless, he must return to Shanghai. He dragged blistered feet eight miles of physical misery, in anger and spiritual rebellion, to the place where he had spent the night in the inn. He managed to bathe his feet, eat, and have four hours' refreshing sleep in the early afternoon.

He walked on, a little less upset, still puzzled. Surely God had intended him to reach Ningpo; it was the obvious course. Why this abandonment? Had he not surrendered home and comfort and safety on God's behalf?

Before the first milestone it dawned on him that he had *denied his Lord*.

Tension suddenly slacked. Anger and pain dissolved in repentance as the truth broke through that he had not asked for guidance or provision before sleeping in the temple steps.

He had lost his temper, thoroughly un-Christlike. He had fussed, worried, forgotten the souls around. He had resented disasters, had expected God to order his affairs as he, Hudson, thought best. "I came as a sinner and pleaded the blood of Jesus, realizing that I was accepted in Him, pardoned, cleansed, sanctified – and oh the love of Jesus, how great I felt it to be."

Hudson Taylor's troubles were not over, but the glorious sense of the love of his Lord swallowed up the miles.

The initiative, the control had passed to Christ – and that was what God had been waiting for.

When at length Taylor reached Shanghai, he received a letter posted in England months earlier which contained a cheque for exactly the amount of his loss. And before long he discovered that had he got through to Ningpo when he had intended, he would have reached Swatow in time to have been imprisoned, perhaps executed.

Words Hudson Taylor wrote at this time come shining through the mist of nearly a hundred and fifty years. "At home you can never know what it is to be alone – absolutely alone, amidst thousands, without one friend, one companion, everyone looking on you with curiosity, with contempt, with suspicion or with dislike. Thus to learn what it is to be despised and rejected of man – of those you wish to benefit, your motives not understood but suspected – thus to learn what it is to have nowhere to lay your head; and then to have the love of Jesus applied to your heart by the Holy Spirit – His holy, self-denying love, which led Him to suffer this and more than this – for *me this is precious*, this is *worth* coming for."

8
The Cambridge Seven – I
Stroke Oar

Stanley Smith 1861–1931

On a bluff April day in 1882 the river banks
of the Thames were crowded once again from
Putney to Mortlake as people watched the annual
Oxford–Cambridge boat race. Cambridge had the
inside station and was away to a good start. But
on the umpire's launch, chugging slowly behind
with a swarming trail of little boats, it was soon
seen that the Cambridge Eight were not together.
By Hammersmith, the Oxford Eight were level, and
excitement was intense. In a few moments they were
ahead and, as Stanley Smith the Cambridge stroke
ruefully remarked, "We were treated to their wash,
after which we went awfully; and finally Oxford won
by seven lengths!"

Though Oxford had won, the critics were loud
in their praise of the Cambridge stroke, who had
given a splendid exhibition of oarsmanship. Three
years later this popular young stroke oar with his
"handsome address and winning manners" was a
humble missionary in China. And the manner of
his going made a stir across the world and lit fires

still burning. The "Cambridge Seven" will never be forgotten.

The event which put S. P. Smith on the road to China was the visit of the American evangelist D. L. Moody to Cambridge University in November 1882. The mission began in derision and ended with "the most remarkable meeting ever seen in Cambridge", a University transformed, and proud undergraduates humbled at the foot of the Cross.

Smith had already finished Cambridge and was working as a schoolmaster in South London. But as a former member of the Cambridge Inter-Collegiate Christian Union C.I.C.C.U., he took leave for the weekend, and was stirred to the depths by what he saw. "Marvellous," he wrote, "verily God's measure is *running over*." Smith had been a Christian since he was twelve. From a fluctuating introspective faith he had passed to settled determination to serve Christ. But it had been on his own terms, with much "insincerity, sham and 'men service'." Never before had he seen God's unfettered power, nor realized his own insignificance.

Though humbled, Stanley Smith had more to learn before God could show him his life's work. The scene changes to a little seaside village on the east coast – Pakefield, Norfolk, on a raw January day two months later. The previous summer Smith had been holiday tutor to the young brother of a Cambridge friend, and had thoroughly enjoyed himself with this Christian family, the Burroughes at Normanstone, near Lowestoft. He had eagerly accepted an invitation to a fortnight's winter visit. The first ten days were much as in the summer

– driving and walking, battledore and shuttlecock,
or word games in the evening; and Bible readings,
hymn singing and evangelistic work among the poor
and navvies. On 18th January Mrs Burroughes and
George were to go on ahead to Burlingham Hall,
George's grandfather's place some fifteen miles
inland, but Harry had wired that he would not
be returning that night, and the three unmarried
daughters would be left alone except for the servants.
Victorian convention demanded that the young bachelor guest must sleep under another roof. Stanley
was to lunch with old Mr Price at Pakefield, and he
walked over with a small handbag to stay the night as
well.

In this trivial manner Smith was led to the second
most decisive experience of his life. Price was a man
of generosity and spirit – an old people's dinner was
proceeding when Stanley arrived, and an evangelistic
meeting followed; but he had discovered also a secret
too little known among Christians in the eighteen-
eighties: "the secret of liberty and delight in the
service of the Lord". He had proved that on a
definite consecration of the whole self to God – not
in intent but in simple deed – the Holy Spirit would
shed abroad the love of God in the heart, producing
a realistic sanctity beyond any previous imagining,
and providing a lasting sense of the presence of the
Lord, "turning your life of duty into a life of liberty
and love".

That night of 18th January, 1883, Price and Stanley
Smith sat up late. As they talked Smith saw something
of the self-will that was hindering him. Because
he enjoyed Christian activities he did them, but

the direction remained in his hands. There were blemishes in his character; and no "hourly abiding", in the presence of Christ, which could only occur, said Price, when Stanley denied himself and took up the Cross, when he handed himself a willing slave unreservedly dedicated to his Master's service, to the Christ who had died to redeem him.

It was after midnight when they went up to their rooms. Stanley Smith had never before seen so vividly the meaning of God's holiness and of his own sin, nor the demands and the possibilities of faith in Christ. Before he got into bed he sat down and wrote in his diary, "I must *fully* consecrate myself".

The next morning they talked again and read Bible passages. Christ was calling, and Smith was in no mind for refusal. Before morning was out he knelt down with Price in the little room in the east coast village, and prayed that the Lord would take his whole life to use it as He wished.

At midday he left Price and walked back to Lowestoft for his navvies' meeting. As he went, "very happy", he found himself singing, "My all is on the altar". At the meeting he experienced a new freedom in speaking. The navvies filled the cramped hall, late-comers content to remain outside in the raw January inshore wind. "His word was with power not mine", wrote Smith. "These dear men with their grasp of the hand and 'God bless you, sir!' repay anything."

"Bless the dear Lord", he could write a few days later "He is in me and *fills* me. How good He is. Oh that all Christians knew this full surrender." Thenceforth his work, his athletics, his friendships

became one unhesitant happy witness to Christ, and
time was spent preaching, and bringing others to
know Christ as Saviour or, knowing Him, to yield
to Him as Lord.

But if Smith thought he was now ready he was
wrong. Clear command for the future was not given
for ten months, until the last day of November 1883.

At a country vicarage in Surrey, close to Leith
Hill, Smith was a speaker at a weekend convention.
During that weekend a verse of Scripture was so
burned into his consciousness that he saw it as a
call from his Lord demanding instant response: "I
will give thee for a light to the Gentiles, that thou
mayst be my salvation unto the end of the earth."

Stanley Smith was in no doubt. It was a call to
foreign service. God was sending him "far hence to
the Gentiles".

Smith's prayers and interest had long followed the
China Inland Mission. Its uncompromising spirituality and its tolerance attracted him as they attracted
Hoste, and it carried the Gospel "not where Christ
was named". Before the end of the year Stanley
Smith had written to the C.I.M. and on 4th January
1884 he went down in the morning to Mildmay,
though suffering from gastric trouble, "to call on Mr
Hudson Taylor of the China Inland Mission. Stayed
till 8 p.m. Had tea there and a nice long talk about
China; I hope to labour for God there soon."

In due course he was accepted. Nor was that
all. Smith felt an urge to awaken others to their
responsibilities to the Christless millions overseas.
Before long, after talks and prayer together, a Cambridge friend joined him – Willie Cassels, a London

curate. Independently a gunner subaltern, D. E. Hoste, was being led along the same road. Two brothers, Arthur and Cecil Polhill-Turner, sons of a wealthy Member of Parliament and country squire, were also sensing the call. Both were former members of the Eton cricket eleven. Arthur was a Cambridge undergraduate, converted through Moody, Cecil a cavalry officer won by his brother.

Smith met them and encouraged them. One of his greatest Cambridge friends Monty Beauchamp, also joined. The climax came with C. T. Studd, the most brilliant all-round cricketer of the day, an Eton, Cambridge, and England player, who in November 1884, after going with Smith to a C.I.M. meeting, determined to leave all and follow Christ to the ends of the earth. . . .

9
The Cambridge Seven – II Test Cricketer

C. T. Studd 1860–1931

C. T. Studd was bred in luxury. His father, Edward Studd, had returned from jute planting at Tirhoor in North India to spend his fortune. At Hallerton in Leicestershire and later at Tedworth House near Andover, the young Studds grew up in a spacious world dedicated to hunting, cricket and their father's fine string of racehorses.

In 1875, when Charlie and his two elder brothers, Kynaston and George, were at Eton, their father's sudden conversion through Moody and Sankey made a startling difference to their lives. Edward Studd now thought only of bringing his friends and family to Christ; as his coachman remarked, "though there's the same skin, there's a new man inside".

The boys had been brought up in the arid formality of conventional religion, "a Sunday thing", so C. T. said later, "like one's Sunday clothes, to be put away on Monday morning". But now his father was "a real live play-the-game Christian". "But it did make one's hair stand on end", was C. T.'s memory, telling the story long afterwards to young people, in the merry way he loved to use. "Everyone in the house had a dog's life of it until they were converted. I was not altogether pleased with him. He used to come into my room at night and ask if I was converted. After a time I used to sham sleep when I saw the door open, and in the day I crept round the other side of the house when I saw him coming."

The following year Edward Studd's prayers were answered. One by one on a single summer's day at Tedworth Hall, each of his three elder sons, J. E. K., G. B., and C. T., all in the Eton eleven, were won for Christ by a guest, a young man called Weatherby, who had earned their respect by his reaction to a cruel practical joke. "Right then and there joy and peace came into my soul," recalled C. T., "I knew then what it is to be 'born again', and the Bible, which had been so dry to me before, became everything."

None of the brothers had courage to tell each other what had happened; it was only disclosed by a joint letter from their father early in the following half at Eton. Edward Studd died shortly afterwards, but Kynaston maintained his tradition, organizing a college Bible Reading. Of C. T., when he left in 1879, his housemaster wrote, "he has done no little good to all who come under his influence". Sport, however, increasingly absorbed his attention. By determination and hard training rather than by native genius he made himself an outstanding all-rounder and was "incomparably the best cricketer" in the Eton and Harrow of 1879, when Captain. He was in the racquets pair, and won the House Fives.

Going up to Trinity in 1879, a freshman with Smith, Beauchamp and William Hoste, Studd won his blue and thus played for Cambridge for four consecutive years, following his brother G. B. as Captain in 1883, to be followed by J. E. K. in 1884. His national fame dated from his great century in 1882 when Cambridge University, against all expectation, defeated the unbeaten Australians. That August, still an undergraduate, twenty-one years old, he played at the Oval in the famous Test Match which England seemed about to win, yet lost to the Australians by eight runs, and the term "The Ashes" was coined. By his Captain's error of judgement in changing the batting order, Studd went in last and never received a ball. The match was so exciting that one spectator gnawed right through the handle of his umbrella.

That year of 1882 C. T. Studd had the highest batting average, and in bowling, though only fifteenth in the averages, had the second highest score of wickets taken. The great W. G. Grace, the Gloucestershire doctor who was the best and most famous cricketer of the Victorian age, described C. T. Studd as "The most brilliant member of a well-known cricketing family, and from 1881 to 1884 he had few superiors as an all-round player. His batting and bowling were very good. . . . His style of batting was free and correct, and he scored largely and rapidly against the best bowlers of his time. He bowled medium-pace, round arm, with a machine-like delivery, and had a fair break from the off."

By 1883 C. T. Studd was a household name, the idol of undergraduates and schoolboys, and the admiration of their elders. But as a Christian he was a nonentity. "Instead of going and telling others of the love of Christ I was selfish and kept the knowledge all to myself. The result was that gradually my love began to grow cold, the love of the world came in." Looking back afterwards he felt he had spent these Cambridge years in one long, "unhappy backsliding state". In fact, he had not been averse to singing "Sankeys" round the piano, or to having a "read and prayer"; he went occasionally to the Daily Prayer Meeting and, as S. P. Smith found, he was willing to take C. I. C. C. U. cards to freshmen. Moreover he was recognized as a Christian, and since cricketing prowess, high spirits, good looks and a kind heart made him outstandingly popular in the University, his identification with the Christian set was not worthless. But he never led another to Christ. Whereas, as he once wrote to Kynaston, "Our cricketing friends used to call you 'The Austere Man' because your life was true to God and you were true to them, for you were ever faithful in speaking to them about their souls", C. T. preferred the easier path. He admired his brother's "courage and loyalty in the Lord Jesus Christ", and was kept by J. E. K.'s influence from utter betrayal of his convictions, but his religion was effete: "mincing, lisping, bated breath, proper", he once described it, "hunting the Bible for hidden truths, but no obedience, no sacrifice".

During Moody's Cambridge mission in the autumn of 1882, C. T. Studd was in Australia with the M. C. C. team which recovered the Ashes, returning in the spring of 1883. By then, S. P. Smith had passed through his great experience of consecration near Lowestoft. Two old ladies, who had known Edward Studd, had set themselves to pray that C. T. be

brought to re-dedication, but their prayers seemed
unanswered. At the end of the 1883 season C. T.
was "for the second year in succession accorded the
premier position as an all-round cricketer. Some
years have elapsed," commented *Wisden's*, "since
the post has been filled by a player so excellent in
all three departments of the game." He was at the
very height of cricketing fame.

At the end of November 1883, when S. P. Smith
was at Brockham in Surrey receiving definite guidance to the Mission Field, C. T.'s brother George,
closest to him in age and affection, fell seriously ill.
C. T. came down from Cambridge in December to
find G. B.'s life in danger. He was prostrate with
grief and anxiety, and as he sat in the sick-room
overlooking the street and narrow gardens, while
carts and carriages rolled softly by over the straw
specially laid down, he began to see life in its true
perspective. At night-time, as he waited in the semi-
darkness lest his brother should call, he "saw what the
world was worth". "As night after night I watched by
the bedside as he was hovering between life and death
God showed me what the honour, what the pleasure,
what the riches of this world were worth. All these
things had become as nothing to my brother. He only
cared about the Bible and the Lord Jesus Christ, and
God taught me the same lesson."

In the first days of January 1884, Studd could
say later, "God brought me back". Very humbly
he reconsecrated himself to his Lord; and as if to
underline that God's hand is in all the accidents
of life, "in His love and goodness He restored my
brother to health". As soon as George was out of

danger, C. T. went to Moody's meeting at St Pancras. "There the Lord met me again and restored to me the joy of my salvation."

Immediately, "and what was better than all", Studd learned the intense satisfaction of spiritual work. He begun to tell his friends of his decision, taking them to Moody or to evangelistic services in Cambridge, devoting himself to Christ with the same determination which he had devoted to cricket. "The Lord was very loving and He soon gave me the consolation of saving one of my nearest and dearest friends. I cannot tell you", he was often to say later, "what joy it gave me to bring the first soul to the Lord Jesus Christ. I have tasted most of the pleasures that this world can give. I do not suppose there was one that I had not experienced; but I can tell you that those pleasures were as nothing compared to the joy that the saving of that one soul gave me."

Back in London for the Easter vacation, after his last term in Cambridge, he was constantly helping at the Moody Campaign. S. P. Smith met him there on Sunday, 23rd March, and they walked back together from St Pancras to Hyde Park Gardens having "a nice talk". The cricket season began and C. T. felt he "must go into the cricket field and get the men there to know the Lord Jesus". He had found "something infinitely better than cricket. My heart was no longer in the game; I wanted to win souls for the Lord." He took members of the Test team to hear Moody. One by one A. J. Webbe, the great batsman, A. G. Steel and Ivo Bligh, the Captain, afterwards Lord Darnley, told Studd that they accepted Christ, and they kept in touch with him for the rest of his life.

On 19th June 1884, the Moody Campaign ended.
The combination of cricket and Christian work had
kept Studd happy without thought for the future.
But now he "wanted to know what my life's work
was to be for the Lord Jesus Christ. I wanted only
to serve Him." Studd was impatient, and conscious
of his powers and influence. It was hard not to
consider himself an asset to the Christian cause
and he expected that he would soon find his niche
and make his mark. No clear guidance, however,
was granted. He invited the opinions of his friends
but they were contradictory. The more he strove to
make up his mind the more impatient he became, and
within a few weeks of Moody's departure Studd had
worked himself into such an emotional tangle that his
health gave way and he had to go into the country to
convalesce.

During July, August and September, while S. P.
Smith, Cassels and Hoste were preparing for China,
C. T. Studd was recovering his balance, spending
much time in Bible study and in prayer for guidance.
His only decision was to read for the Bar "until the
Lord Jesus should show me what my life's work was
to be for Him". As soon as he returned to Hyde Park
Gardens early in October even this decision seemed
wrong, and he was convinced that he must spend
his whole time in Christian service. His inheritance
was ample, "God had given me far more than was
sufficient to keep body and soul together. . . . How
could I spend the best hours of my life in working
for myself and for the honour and pleasures of this
world while thousands and thousands of souls are
perishing every day without having heard of the Lord

Jesus Christ, going down to Christless and hopeless graves?"

Studd's mind worked in single tracks. Whatever he did must be done to the utter exclusion of other interests. Awakened as he was, he knew that nothing less than uninhibited dedication to the winning of souls would satisfy him. He "began to read the Bible more earnestly and to ask God what I was to do. But this time I determined not to consult with flesh and blood, but just wait until God should show me."

But the first thing God had to show him was himself. Towards the end of September a close friend invited Studd to a drawing-room Bible meeting. A passage was read. As they studied it someone mentioned a woman they all knew. "Have you heard of the extraordinary blessing Mrs W. has received? . . . You know she has been an earnest Christian worker for nearly her whole life, and has had a good deal of trouble and sorrow which has naturally weighed upon her. But somehow lately God has given her such a blessing that although she has had so much trial it does not affect her at all now. Nothing seems to trouble her. She lives a life of perfect peace." They turned to their Bibles again to see whether such a blessing was promised. Before they parted they were convinced that the peace which "passeth understanding" and "joy unspeakable" were offered to every Christian, and they had knelt down to ask that God should "give us this blessing".

Back in his own room Studd knelt down again, "very much in earnest". Someone had just given him a popular American book, *The Christian's Secret of a Happy Life. The Christian's Secret*, by Hannah Pearsall Smith, which was to become a best seller when published in England four years later, dealt in simple, practical terms with the very possibilities which they had been discussing at the Bible meeting. "In order to enter into this blessed interior life of rest and triumph," wrote Mrs Pearsall Smith, "you have two steps to take – first, entire abandonment, and second, absolute faith." As Studd read, sometimes on his knees and sometimes sitting in his chair, he began to see that he had not received the blessing because he had been "keeping back from God what belonged to Him". "I had known about Jesus Christ's dying for me, but I had never understood that if he died for me, then I didn't belong to myself. Redemption means 'buying back', so that if I belonged to Him, either I had to be a thief and keep what wasn't mine, or else I had to give up everything to God. When I came to see that Jesus Christ had died for me, it didn't seem hard to give up all for HIM. It seemed just common, ordinary honesty."

Convinced that "I had kept back myself from Him, and had not wholly yielded", C.T. Studd went down on his knees and from the bottom of his heart said the words of Frances Ridley Havergal's hymn

> "Take my life and let it be
> Consecrated, Lord, to Thee."

The next step was faith – a straightforward confidence that God had accepted his life because it was offered, and that what He had taken He could keep. Then and there Studd took up the position which was to be his chief characteristic to the day he died: "I realized that my life was to be one of simple, childlike faith. . . . I was to trust in Him that He would work in me to do His good pleasure. I saw that He was my loving Father and that He would guide me and keep me, and moreover that He was well able to do it."

What S.P. Smith had discovered near Lowestoft in January 1883, C.T. Studd found in London in September 1884 – peace, security, overflowing contentment and a willingness to go wherever he was sent.

It was not long before light was thrown on the future. Until his recent experience no thought of overseas service had crossed Studd's mind: "England was big enough for me." But the call of the foreign field soon became insistent. It was almost a matter of mere mathematics – the percentage of Christless people to every witnessing Christian. Furthermore, the pioneer's blood was stirring in his veins. As for sacrifice, it seemed the wrong word to express the intensity of his joy in being put to God's work.

On Saturday, 1st November, Stanley Smith returned to London from his farewell visits to Cambridge and Oxford. His contacts had been informal – frequent, crowded meetings in the colleges, breakfasts and lunches with twos or threes, brief words at Bible Readings and prayer meetings. At about eleven o'clock in the morning of that Saturday, on his way home from Paddington Station to John Street, Stanley Smith drove up in a hansom cab to Number Two Hyde Park Gardens, to call at the Studds'. Both Kynaston and C.T. were in, and when Smith mentioned that he was going that evening to

the C.I.M. headquarters to a service of farewell to
John McCarthy, a returning missionary, C.T. said
he would join him.

At the service McCarthy, one of the founder
members of the C.I.M., told once again the story
of his call, nearly twenty years before, and spoke of
the vastness of spiritual need in China, "thousands of
souls perishing every day and night without even the
knowledge of the Lord Jesus". As McCarthy spoke,
C.T. Studd was convinced that God "was indeed
leading me to China".

As McCarthy's address closed and they were singing *He leadeth me*, Studd for a moment thought of
rising in his place and offering for China on the
spot. But he felt "people would say I was led
by impulse". When the meeting ended he slipped
away by himself and prayed for guidance. Only one
consideration made him hesitate: he cared not at
all that to bury himself in China would end his
cricket and snuff out his national reputation, that
it might invite the disapproval of worldly friends;
as for hardship, he relished the prospect. But he
knew that his mother would be heart-broken. Should
he repay her love by deserting her? Could he
face wounding one to whom he was devoted? He
opened his pocket Bible. A passage in Matthew
10 seemed to answer his doubts: "He that loveth
father or mother more than me is not worthy of
me". At that he "knew it was God's wish he should
go".

Studd told no one at the meeting. On the way
home, as the two young men sat well wrapped up on
the open top of the horse-bus clattering down Essex

Road, Studd told Smith that he had "decided to go to China".

Stanley Smith was so delighted at the news that on reaching John Street, after parting from Studd, he decided, late as it was, to return to the C.I.M. at Mildmay and break the news to McCarthy and to write to Hudson Taylor, who was away in the country. For Smith and his friends the night of 1st November ended in praise and thanksgiving.

For Studd it ended in conflict. He immediately reported his decision to Kynaston. Kynaston, who knew what it would mean to their mother and who could not forget Charlie's aberrations during the past four months, doubted the validity of the guidance. C.T. broke the news to Mrs. Studd. As he had feared, she was distraught.

The next two days were a nightmare. "I never saw anything like Kinny's depression," wrote Monty Beauchamp, who was round there on the Monday night, 3rd November, "he says he has never in his life seen two such days of suffering and sorrow, referring to his mother. . . . All day she was imploring Charlie not to go up to Mildmay and at all events just to wait one week before giving himself to H. Taylor. He would listen to no entreaties from Mrs Studd or Kynaston, who looked upon him as a kind of fanatic." That Monday night Kynaston determined on one last effort: "Charlie, I think you are making a great mistake. You are away every night at the meetings and don't see your mother. I see her, and this is just breaking her heart." "Let us ask God," replied C. T., "I don't want to be pigheaded and go out there of my own accord. I just want to do God's will." J.

E. K.'s advice and help had always meant much, and "it was hard to have him think it was a mistake". They knelt and put the whole matter in God's hands. "That night," said C. T. later, "I could not get to sleep, but it seemed as though I heard someone say these words over and over, 'Ask of me, and I shall give thee the heathen for thine inheritance and the uttermost parts of the earth for thy possession'".(Psalm 2.8).

This verse convinced him. On Tuesday, 4th November, he set his face to Mildmay, called on Hudson Taylor and was accepted. The conflict was not yet over. As, once again, the horse-bus trotted down the dimly-lit Essex Road, the entreaties of his brother and his mother's weeping were uppermost in C. T.'s mind. Having held out so long, he was tempted to waver and withdraw his offer to the Mission. He alighted at King's Cross Underground Railway station, and stood on the platform waiting for the Bayswater train to steam in. In despair he prayed for a sure word of guidance. He drew out his pocket Bible. With a platform lamp flickering over his shoulder he opened and read: "A man's foes shall be they of his own houshold." With that his way was clear – and when Mrs Studd knew that C. T. was settled in his decision she withdrew her opposition and supported him warmly for the rest of her life.

10
The Cambridge Seven – III
A Torch is Lit

The announcement that Studd was going to China caused immense excitement in the universities.

Not only was C. T. Studd a household name, but the suddenness of his decision seemed to make it the more impressive. Smith had been stumping the country for Christ for nearly two years. Studd had been absorbed by cricket. "We never thought he would go", was an Eton friend's comment. Moreover his sacrifice, abandoning cricket at the height of his fame, was the more apparent. Oxford undergraduates crowded to hear him.

"You have no idea how wonderfully the Lord helped and blessed dear Studd", wrote Smith to "My dear Mr Hudson Taylor" after the first meeting. "We were simply so full of the joy of the Lord we could only wear the broadest grins on our faces for the rest of the night!"

They spent six days at Oxford, two others joining for the last day. Curiously, in view of what was to happen, the later meetings were not well attended, and at one time Smith and his friends endured a sharp attack of depression and doubt.

At Cambridge, where Smith, Studd and Monty Beauchamp were to speak, the effect was marked. As one undergraduate said afterwards, "We have had missionary meetings and we have been hearing missionaries talk to us from time to time. But when men whom everybody had heard of and many had known personally came up and said, 'I am going out myself', we were brought face to face with the heathen abroad."

Each day enthusiasm rose. Though some of the dons criticized Smith and Studd for their lack of scholarship, and the more flippant undergraduates wrote them off as eccentric, the Christian Union men were stirred to the depths. Smith won their hearts by his charm and shook them from complacency by the fervour of his call, supported by Studd in clipped, homely phrases. As the men listened to these "spiritual millionaires", as one undergraduate described them, the very content of the word "sacrifice" seemed reversed: and each man wondered whether he could afford the cost, not of utter devotion and worldly loss but of compromise and the loss of spiritual power and joy. Nothing less than the experience of these two men was worth having.

During this week the two brothers Polhill – Turner became certain that they were called too; both had been feeling their way, Arthur to give up (or postpone) ordination, Cecil to resign his cavalry commission. Cecil had already called on Hudson Taylor. When Arthur realized that Cecil might be joining the five others, he sensed a challenge that he, too, should join them.

. . . . .

Smith and Studd's Cambridge mission had increased
the "extraordinary interest aroused by the announcement that the captain of the Cambridge eleven and
the stroke oar of the Cambridge boat were going out
as missionaries". The news was in everyone's mouth,
competing in public interest with the national anxiety
for Gordon in Khartoum. These two young men, the
world at their feet, seemed to be sacrificing so much
so early to bury themselves in the back of beyond.
And, by all accounts, they were doing it with gusto.
"S.P." and "C.T." were daily discovering the depths
and heights of grace. "Dear Charlie is as full of
blessing as an egg is of meat", wrote Smith on
23rd November, while Smith spoke for himself of
the "glorious liberty Christ has won for me". Both
had told Hudson Taylor that their personal wealth
was at the Mission's disposal.

Hudson Taylor had intended to set off early in
January 1885 with a miscellaneous party including
Hoste, Smith and Cassels. But as his son and
daughter-in-law wrote in their biography, "the unexpected happened, and God's purposes broke in
upon these well-laid plans with an over-flowing ful-
ness which carried all before it".

The human agent was an elderly and noted evangelist living in Liverpool, Reginald Radcliffe, a close
friend of Hudson Taylor. Radcliffe had noted Studd's
and Smith's influence on students and had a particular
desire to extend it to Scotland. With Hudson Taylor's
permission he had written to Professor Alexander

Simpson of Edinburgh, a distinguished throat special-
ist and layman, suggesting a visit by the two young
men.

On 28th November, Smith and Studd left by the
night train from Euston for Glasgow – Studd with
nothing but the clothes he stood up in. His mother
was very distressed, when Taylor asked her to send
a parcel, "at my son Charlie's erratic movements
and going off to Scotland without any clothes of
any sort except those he had on. How or why he
should wear one shirt night and day till the 9th
of December is a mystery to me when he has a
supply provided, and one has always been taught
that 'Cleanliness is next to Godliness'." She urged
Taylor to place him, in China, with an older and
sober minded Christian in steady work. "I feel
that he and Mr Stanley Smith are too much of
the same impulsive nature and one excites the
other."

On 2nd December, Studd's twenty-fourth birthday,
they spoke to Glasgow University students. After
brief visits elsewhere they arrived in Edinburgh.
Studd and Smith were not taking this tour in their
stride. "When we went round the students," wrote
Studd later, "we were in a mortal funk about meeting
them because we had never done anything like this.
So we used to stay sometimes all night by the fire on
the mat, sometimes praying and sometimes sleeping."
And thus in the meetings, as Smith could write, "there
was much power".

At Edinburgh all was ready. But even Stanley
Smith and C. T. could scarcely have expected the
result.

A committee of professors and students had sent
sandwich-men tramping the neighbourhood and had
circulated printed notices. They had taken the Free
Assembly Hall, a large building holding a thousand,
and challenged their own faith by announcing that
students only would be admitted.

Nevertheless they were afraid. This was the age
of strident rationalism; Edinburgh University was
largely medical and, despite the impact made by
Moody three years earlier, Christianity was at a
discount and considered "only good for psalm-singing
and pulling a long face". "There were two fears," said
one of the organizers, "the first – that there would
not be a meeting; the second – that if there should
be, there would be a 'row' – a very common thing
amongst Scottish students."

Studd and Stanley Smith spent the bleak December
afternoon in their host's drawing room "in prayer, till
they got victory".

In the University, as the evening drew on, "the
word went round our class-rooms, 'Let us go and give
a welcome to the athlete missionaries'." Well before
the hour the hall was crammed. As the committee
and speakers knelt in the green-room they could hear
the students "singing their usual before lecture songs
and beating time with their sticks", but Studd shamed
the fears of the organizers by calmly thanking God for
the result and, as one of them wrote, "we felt there
was going to be a great blessing."

The two "athlete missionaries" entered the hall
and were warmly cheered. A divinity professor, Dr
Charteris, a Chaplain to the Queen, took the chair.
C. T. Studd spoke first, then R.J. Landale, an Oxford

man returned from China, and lastly Smith. "Stanley Smith was eloquent," one of the students recalled years later, "but Studd couldn't speak a bit – it was the fact of his devotion to Christ which told, and he, if anything, made the greatest impression." Again and again he was cheered. "The fact that a man with such prospects as he should thus devote himself and his fortune gave them an interest in him from the very first", wrote the chairman. It was an age of ponderous homilies, and by the very contrast of Studd's happy, ungarnished story of spiritual development "the students were spellbound".

Landale's talk was on China, and Stanley Smith then began. Taking as his text "They feared the Lord, and served their own gods", he showed up, "in words of burning scorn", the flat, effete selfishness which so often passed for Christian service. He was heard in utter stillness. "As he spoke," said one of the committee, "our hearts condemned us." The atmosphere was tense with spiritual power. Smith swept on, his "unusual powers of thought, imagination and utterance" roused to highest pitch by the response of his audience.

When he had done, the chairman announced that any who would "like to shake hands with them and wish them Godspeed" could come forward after the Benediction. The committee expected that few would have sufficient courage in front of other students. To their amazement, "no sooner had the Benediction been pronounced than there was a stampede to the platform". Nor was it mere curiosity. "They were crowding round Studd and Smith to hear more about Christ; deep earnestness was written on the faces of many. . . . It was all so evidently the work of the Holy Spirit."

The meeting closed and Studd and Smith returned to their host's for a meal before catching the night mail to London. Shortly before half-past ten the two walked down to Waverley Station with a medical professor and several students, who were urging them to return before they left for China. At the station a hundred students or more were waiting. "Speech! Speech!" they cried as the two men appeared. Studd stood on a seat and said a few words, resoundingly cheered. The quiet station had seen nothing like it since Gladstone's Midlothian Campaign five years before. A traveller asked what the fuss was about. "Th're a meedical students," replied a porter, "but th're aff their heeds!"

As the train steamed out into the night Smith and Studd were waving from the carriage windows, some of the students running to the end of the platform, cheering and shouting goodbye, while others stood singing "God be with you till we meet again".

.   .   .   .   .   .

On the evening of 8th January 1885 the Seven were together for the first time on the platform of the Exeter Hall, supporting Hudson Taylor. Though nothing to what was to come, the hall was "absolutely packed". The Polhill-Turners both spoke of their call, and Stanley Smith wound up a long meeting with a comparatively short address. From that evening "the Cambridge Seven" became a household name.

The next day Studd and Smith left Euston by the
1.30 p.m. express for Liverpool. Reginald Radcliffe
met them, and they began the same evening with
a meeting of young men. "A most remarkable
one", wrote Smith. "About twelve hundred there
– packed: and such a time of power. Many received
Jesus. Young men broken down; I hear there were
seventy or more awakened. This is the Lord's
doing."

After meetings in six Scottish cities the two came
to Edinburgh and found two thousand students were
awaiting them, "the largest meeting of students that
has ever been held" in Edinburgh. "I lifted up Christ
crucified," wrote Smith simply, "and Charlie gave
his testimony." None there could afterwards forget,
as Dr Moxey of the divinity faculty wrote, Smith's
"big muscular hands and long arms stretched out in
entreaty while he eloquently told out the old story
of redeeming love", or Studd's "quiet but intense
and burning utterances of personal testimony to
the love and power of a personal Saviour". More
than half the hall stayed for counselling. On the
Monday when they had spoken with equal effect to
two further audiences, they promised to return after
their engagements in Glasgow; and on the Friday
they were back, to learn that all the signs of religious
revival were about.

Their final meeting with the Edinburgh students
proved the most remarkable. Many were in tears
before the end, and three or four hundred stayed
to the after meeting. At half past ten the floor was
still "covered with men anxiously enquiring 'What
must I do to be saved?'" One of the committee

sought out the manager and obtained an extension
of lease till midnight, and up to the end could be
seen "the glorious sight of professors dealing with
students and students with one another". As for
Smith and Studd, they were utterly humbled. "There
were several conversions," was all Smith could find
in him to say, "and many began to yield to God what
had long been His due."

.   .   .   .   .   .

Newcastle, Manchester, Rochdale, Leeds – through
the smoke-grimed cities of the North, Smith and
Studd moved in a triumphal tour, though the triumph
was not theirs but Christ's. At Manchester on 26th
January, "a most glorious meeting," wrote Stanley
Smith, "nearly all young men. Fully a thousand
stayed to the after-meeting: and going away we
did have our hands squeezed, a somewhat painful
show of friendship!" At Rochdale, the next day,
they had "a most remarkable meeting. Quite the
most remarkable." Studd's comment was more pic-
turesque. "We had a huge after-meeting," he wrote
to his mother, "it was like a charge of dynamite
exploded among them."

Wherever they went the effect was the same.
Young men of all classes flocked to hear them.
In the early eighteen eighties wealth and position
could command a respect untinged with envy, while
the testimony of the greatest all-round cricketer in
England, supported by a prominent oarsman, could
impress where other men's words fell flat. And
because of the imminent sacrifice of all that the

world held dear, many could take from Studd and
Smith what they would not from older men whose
calling, however rightly, was conducted from cosy
vicarages. Studd and Smith were the men for the
hour.

They knew well enough that they were neither
better nor more important than other Christian
workers, but because they had yielded all they
were given all. "I cannot tell you how very much
the Lord has blessed us," wrote Studd to his mother,
"and we daily grow in the knowledge of Jesus and
His wonderful love; what a different life from my
former one; why, cricket and racquets and shooting
are nothing to this overwhelming joy." Furthermore,
their conscience was stirred to the depths by the
North, still in the throes of the industrial depression
of the early 'eighties. "Finding out so much about the
poor in the great towns", wrote Studd, "has increased
my horror at the luxurious way I have been living; so
many suits and clothes of all sorts, whilst thousands
are starving and perishing of cold, so all must be
sold when I come home if they have not been so
before."

On Thursday, 29th January, Studd, Smith and
Radcliffe came back to where they had started a
fortnight before, reaching Liverpool early in the
afternoon. After a brief rest at the Radcliffes', out
at Waterloo, they came in for the final meeting at
the Y.M.C.A. "Packed, and an overflow pretty full."
The two were told afterwards that sixty young men
had "professed conversion on that one night".

Shortly before eleven the two jumped into a cab for
Lime Street Station. Symbolically, at the end of such

a whirlwind tour, the cab horse "ran away with us and bolted down Pembroke Place, though fortunately no damage was done"

After reaching London in a cheerless drizzle in the dark of the early morning, and spending the day quietly at their homes, Stanley Smith and C.T. Studd joined the others on the evening of Friday, 30th January, for the C.I.M.'s final London Farewell at the Eccleston Hall. Hudson Taylor had left England the previous week.

From then on, except for a rushed visit by Studd and Smith at the weekend to Bristol, where the Colston Hall was not large enough for those who came to hear them, the Cambridge Seven were together – at Cambridge, Oxford, and a final public meeting at Exeter Hall, the historic London rendez-vous of evangelicals – three meetings which burned the message of the Seven into the consciousness of the nation.

"When before", asked one religious newspaper, "were the stroke of a University eight, the captain of a University eleven, an officer of the Royal Artillery, an officer of the Dragoon Guards, seen standing side by side renouncing the careers in which they had already gained no small distinction, putting aside the splendid prizes of earthly ambition . . . and plunging into that warfare whose splendours are seen only by faith and whose rewards seem so shadowy to the unopened vision of ordinary men?" Yet the crowds did not come to flatter or gape. "Spirituality", recalled Eugene Stock of the C. M. S., "marked most emphatically the densely crowded meetings at which these seven men said farewell. They told, modestly and yet fearlessly, of the Lord's goodness to them, and of the joy of serving Him; and they appealed to young men, not for their Mission, but for the divine Master."

The Cambridge Seven attracted not only by their birth and athletic prowess, and by the sacrifice they were evidently making, but because they were not cut to a pattern. Smith and Studd were ascetics, reacting violently from the comfort of their early lives. The Polhill-Turners, no less devoted, did not make such sharp distinctions. "C. T. believed in rigid austerity," wrote Cecil Polhill later, describing a journey in China, "and no comfort of any sort, either of furniture or luxury in food were for a moment allowed. He would not allow himself even a back to a chair. My brother was mildly ascetic. ... To me it did not matter one way or the other, all was good, and so we hit it off capitally." Hoste and Cassels were both fastidious men, though going to the squalor of China with as much readiness as Cassels had gone to the slums.

At first meeting, Smith would seem severe, though affectionate and charming on closer acquaintance, but Studd's gentleness almost belied his burning words. Beauchamp, with his enormous frame and somewhat florid face, and his capacity to extract enjoyment from anything, was almost as eloquent as Smith; but Hoste and Cecil Polhill-Turner were shy and found public speaking a trial. Cassels, as quiet as Hoste, as good a speaker as Beauchamp, was in many ways the most mature of them all.

"*Exeter Hall* – last night, what shall I say? Such a meeting!" wrote the C.I.N Secretary to Hudson Taylor next morning. "I question if a meeting of equal significance and spiritual fruitfulness has been held in that building during this generation. Its influence upon the cause of missions must be immense, incalculable."

"It was a most magnificent success," he went on. "Exeter Hall was packed in every part, and people of note and title had to get in anywhere and be thankful if they got in at all . . . That meeting will be the talk of all England wherever men meet who are interested in the cause of missions."

Rain had been falling hard all evening, but "long before the time announced", reported *The Times*, "the large hall was crowded in every part, and an overflow meeting of some of the many unable to obtain admission was held in the small hall". "Over three thousand," Stanley Smith was told, "and the overflow five hundred, besides hundreds going away." Dr Barnardo and other well-known figures had to stand the entire time.

The meeting had been arranged for young men but they were lost in a miscellaneous mass of men and women "of all sections of the Church and grades of social life".

Stanley Smith spoke first and longest and held his audience spell-bound. ". . . We do not go to that far distant field to speak of doctrine or theory, but of a living, bright, present and rejoicing Saviour," not to offer "the milk-and-water of religion but the cream of the Gospel, and to tell what a blessed thing it was to have the love of the Lord Jesus Christ reigning in low hearts."

When he reached his peroration the stillness was profound. "How can one leave such an audience as this? It seems to me as if Christ has come right into your midst, and has looked into the face of you men and women, young, old and middle-aged. He would take hold with loving hands of each one, and looking into your eyes point to the wounds in His pierced side, and ask 'Lovest thou me?' And you would say, 'Yea, Lord, thou knowest that I love thee.' And what is the test of love? 'If you love me keep my commandments.' And what, Master, do you command? 'Go ye into all the world and preach the Gospel to every creature.'"

Five of the Seven spoke more briefly. Then C.T. Studd rose. "I want to recommend you tonight to my Master. I have tried many ways of pleasure in my time; I have been running after the best master – and, thank God, I have found Him." Unhurriedly, without flourish or effect, he told the story of "how the Lord has sought and found me and led me back to Himself." The simplicity of the narrative, coming from such a man as Studd, brought the challenge of Christ to every man and woman present. "What are you really living for?", he concluded, "Are you living for the day or are you living for the life eternal? Are you going to care for the opinion of men here, or for the opinion of God? The opinion of men won't avail us much when we get before the judgement throne. But the opinion of God will. Had we not, then, better take His word and implicitly obey it?"

Next day the Cambridge Seven left London for China.

.   .   .   .   .

"There is enough power in this meeting to stir not only London and England but the whole world", said the eminent Nonconformist who gave the closing address at Exeter Hall.

The interest was enormous. Fifty thousand copies of the China Inland Mission's account of the meetings were sold, and a revised edition a year later, with additional material sent back by the Seven from China, became a best seller. In Britain, universities experienced a revival which spread to American colleges and led to the formation of the Student Volunteer Missionary Union, ancestor of the great evangelical student movements of the twentieth century throughout the world.

As for the Cambridge Seven themselves, their paths diverged but not one looked back, and a high proportion of their children (all the seven married) became missionaries in their turn.

Stanley Smith's life was spent in North China. He became a fine linguist and as fluent a preacher in Chinese as in English. In later years he endured severe trials and disappointments but worked on until the end, preaching and teaching until the night before he died on 31st January 1931.

C. T. Studd was the best known of the Seven in later life. His courage and endurance were unquenchable.

In 1887, determined to live by faith alone, he gave away the whole of his fortune. His mother and family disapproved but when he married and had four daughters, they nobly paid for their education.

In 1894, broken in health, Studd and his wife left China, never to return. After six years in India and a period in Britain and America, where his words did much for the missionary cause, Studd set off in 1910 into the depths of tropical Africa, pioneering in defiance of illness, criticism and poverty. From his faith grew the Worldwide Evangelization Crusade, and though in later years he became a controversial figure, nothing could detract from the splendour of C.T. Studd's witness to Christ. Studd died at Ibambi, Belgian Congo, on 16th July 1931, over a thousand Africans seeing him to his grave.

The last of the Seven, D.E. Hoste, who had succeeded Hudson Taylor as leader of the China Inland Mission in 1903, died in London in 1946, but long after the later lives of the men who formed it are forgotten the Cambridge Seven will remain in the consciousness of the Christian Church – their splendid sacrifice, and their wholehearted devotion to the call of Christ; their intolerance of shoddy spirituality in themselves or in others, and their grasp of the urgency of the Gospel to unevangelized millions overseas.

And, particularly relevant, not one of the Seven was a genius. Theirs is a story of ordinary men, and thus may be repeated, not only in countries of the West but in lands which were the mission fields of a century ago but now send missionaries themselves.

The Gospel of Christ is unchanged, and His call is unchanged. The Cambridge Seven illustrate how that call may be heard: "God does not deal with you until you are wholly given up to Him, and then He will tell you what He would have you do."

11
The Good Gossips of Gobi

Mildred Cable 1878–1952
Eva and Francesca French
1869–1960 and 1871–1960

"We sat for hours leaning back against the Great Wall of China, as our cart was up to the axle in a mud pit." All efforts by the two mules had failed. The three Western women in Chinese dress, with their faithful servant and the Chinese doctor's wife and little girl, could only hope that someone would pass by. Their incompetent carter, hired that morning to drive them the last stage, had given up.

At last they heard a movement behind the crumbling Wall. The head of an ox emerged, fixing "wondering and meditative eyes upon us sitting there". As the ox lumbered through the opening a man rode up on a donkey. The donkey stopped, transfixed at the sight of cart, women and ox, and "sank peacefully to the ground as if in a state of mental collapse", so that its rider had no option but to dismount and help them. The carter caught the ox; the traveller hitched his donkey to the mules; ox, donkey and mules heaved together, while the men and the ladies pushed. The cart squelched out of the mud.

Their large white mule, Lolly, and a beautiful little brown called Molly, drew them slowly forward in the teeth of a March wind, through a desolate countryside with distant mountains on both horizons. A sleet storm lashed their faces; the carter stuck them in the mud again; they feared they would never reach the city of Kanchow, in the remote north-west of China, by nightfall.

Suddenly they saw two horsemen galloping towards them – the Chinese Christian doctor and a friend. Dr Kao greeted them with joy and then turned to the carter. "Hullo, Old Sheep! You out of jail again?"

The cart was dragged out of the mud; the second horseman galloped back towards the city while the doctor escorted the four women and the little girl. Before dusk a relay of fine horses, belonging to a Mongol prince who was staying with the doctor, came out to their rescue and they rode through the gate of Kanchow into darkened streets, past flaring smithies and busy inns, to the doctor's compound "and a longed-for cup of tea".

The three Western ladies had embarked on a great adventure for Christ. They had already been many years in China. Eva French, aged nearly fifty-four when they reached Kanchow in March 1924, had joined the China Inland Mission before the Boxer Rising of 1900, in which she had nearly lost her life. She was Irish, and had been somewhat wild in her girlhood, but her temperament owed more to Calvin's Geneva, where she had been brought up. Mildred Cable, nine years younger, had joined her in 1902; she was a draper's daughter from Surrey, who had trained as a pharmacist. At great emotional cost

she had broken off an engagement when forced to
choose between marriage and the mission field, yet
she was cheerful, always ready to laugh, and strongly
drawn to pioneering. Eva's sister, Francesca, had
come to China later, after their mother had died:
she was between the other two in age and had some
training as a nurse.

They spent nearly twenty years together in a
flourishing mission station in North China, much
loved for their gifts of spontaneous friendship with
all whom they met. The Chinese called Eva the
Grey Lady, Mildred the Blue Lady, and Francesca
the Brown Lady. Towards the end of the Great War,
which hardly touched life in China, the Trio began to
feel an urge to break away and go where few or none
had heard of Christ. Their thoughts centred on the
remote provinces of Kansu, Sinkiang and Mongolia.
They had "a secret consciousness of being in receipt
of 'Sealed Orders', marked '*To proceed to the Great
North-west to a place at present unknown*'."

And thus, in June 1923, to the tears of the large
congregation, they set out on the long journey up
the great Silk Road, with a first stock of New
Testaments in Chinese, Turku and other tongues.
Dr Kao, who had pioneered a Christian hospital and
church in Kanchow, had invited them to begin their
adventure there. By unhurried stages, evangelizing
as they went, staying in the filthy inns which were all
that the road could offer, they reached Kanchow in
March 1924.

At Dr Kao's suggestion they first trained a band of
young Christian men and women, and then travelled
up and down the region, holding meetings in a tent

which the young men would erect and dismantle. At that time – for a period all too short – the country was peaceful and the courteous people listened. But the Trio had no desire to settle. The Gobi Desert beckoned: the oases with their Tartars and Turkus; the trade routes leading from Tibet, Mongolia and Turkestan. Beyond Kanchow lay Suchow, the last walled city before the Great Wall and the desert, known as the City of Prodigals because of its fugitives from debt, justice, or stepmothers.

The Trio, accompanied by a pioneer band who would form the nucleus of a Bible school and church, were able to rent a delightful house in a garden with a glorious view of distant snow mountains in Tibet, but the Gobi made its presence felt when the wind swept in through their paper windows "deluging us with grit as we lay in our beds. When daylight came, we found our room literally buried under a thick layer of Gobi Desert dust, and for forty-eight hours the fearful blast persisted."

Suchow would be their headquarters: the Gobi Desert their field. No Europeans had traversed it since Marco Polo, except a few destitute Russian refugees and the eminent explorer, Sir Aurel Stein. The Trio were as interested as Stein in the extraordinary contours and colours of the largest desert on earth; in the Cave of a Thousand Buddhas, and the lamaseries and temples of the great oases. They took copious notes which were later to be basis of their fame. But their plain object was to tell the scattered people of the Gobi about Christ, and to place in the hands of wayfarers, wherever they came from, the New Testament and gaily illustrated Christian books in a tongue they could understand.

Eva Mildred and Francesca would plan carefully and set out in the cart drawn by Lolly and Molly at three miles an hour, to reach an oasis town, perhaps days away, during a fair or a religious festival.

"Lama, you look tired", Mildred would say. "Yes," replied the man, "I have walked eight months to get here. I have come from the east, seeking the land where the sun sets and where I can find God."

Eva spoke to a temple priest: "You have had a busy day!"

'Yes, and you also, I believe, and I have not had time to come and listen to you. What is it that brings you so far?"

"Have you ever heard of Jesus?"

"Yes, I did hear of Him once, in a temple, where the priest said that he believed in Jesus of Nazareth." Mildred and Francesca came across, and a long and courteous discussion continued far into the night.

The Trio called their work "Gossiping the Gospel", pointing out that the word *gossip* derives, like gospel, from the Anglo-Saxon word *God-spell*; a gossip was a *God's sip*, or "Friend of the Lord", who talked about Him to a pagan and then stood as the *gossip* or sponsor at the baptism which followed when the pagan had accepted Christ. The Trio talked to any who came near their book table, such as the Chinese merchant commanding a long string of camels loaded with his merchandise. He bought and carried off, "like a great treasure", a complete Bible in Chinese, glad to have a good read for the long lonely stages.

Soon afterwards came a man from Mongolia on a swift camel, singing at the top of his voice. His large sheepskin garment probably hid a bag of gold dust, enough to buy their whole stock, "but this time it is not money that we are out for. What we want of him is an unconscious act of colportage, so that when he leaves us and rides away his capacious saddle bags will hold many of those books provided for us by the Bible Society. Lamas all along his way will beg for a volume and offer hospitality in return." Furthermore, his homeland and journey's end was closed to missionaries but the books could enter in his bags.

Mildred, Eva and Francesca were confident that "the Glad Sound" (Chinese for the Gospel) can "take hold on a man's mind so that it dominates his thought for life". They could not go everywhere themselves but "the Word of God is not bound". And sometimes they rejoiced to find a heart already prepared. Near the celebrated Crescent Moon Lake they met a Tibetan lama on pilgrimage. "He surprised us by saying that this meeting caused him no surprise: 'This Jesus of whom you speak has appeared to me several times in a dream. I know that I have to believe in Him.'"

.   .   .   .   .   .

Back in Suchow, one winter day, Mildred opened the door to find a small girl in rags, with cuts and bruises on her legs, holding out a begging bag.

"Where do you come from, child?", asked Mildred.

The girl merely pointed to the dog bites on her legs. Mildred soon realized that the child, who looked about seven or eight, was deaf and dumb. "*What* a poor mite!" she exclaimed as Eva came out to look, followed by Francesca with a bowl of soup which the child wolfed. Then Mildred bandaged her sores.

Next day a garishly dressed woman tried to extort money from the Trio for "letting their dog bite her little daughter". Their cook, who recognized the woman as a bad lot, told her roundly that the household had no dog and that she should be ashamed of herself. The woman changed her tune and said she would thrash the child for misleading her, at which Eva threatened to report her to the mandarin: a well dressed woman had no business to drive her child to beg and be bitten by watch dogs which other beggar children would hear and avoid. The woman left quickly.

Mildred nicknamed the child *Gwa Gwa*, "Little Lonely", and after enquiries by their neighbour, Granny Fan, discovered that the child was a slave, not a daughter. Some eight years earlier a Mongol chieftain, joining in the revelry at a festival in the Tibetan foothills, had slaked his lust on a peasant girl and ridden away with no further thought. He had sired a girl, unwanted but beautiful, and at the age of three weeks easily sold in Suchow to a childless woman. But when the child grew she was found to be stone deaf and mute. Her foster mother, furious at the bad bargain, took away her pretty clothes, dressed her in rags and later drove her out to beg.

Gwa Gwa took to calling regularly at this house, where no dog bit, and where a bowl of soup and a hunk of bread, and kind smiles, were always to be found. But the Trio were due for furlough. Gwa Gwa instinctively realized that they would be gone a long time (though the Christians would see that she did not starve), and she followed their cart out of the city until Mildred, as miserable as Gwa Gwa at the parting, stopped the cart and gently persuaded her to turn back.

The Trio had planned their furlough in character. They would go home to England slowly across the Gobi Desert by their own cart, "the Gobi Express" as they jocularly called it, gossiping the Gospel at oases familiar or new, until they crossed the pass into Sinkiang, and thus to its capital Urumchi, eight hundred miles from Suchow.

At Urumchi they stayed with the veteran missionary George Hunter, and left Molly the Mule as his guest, then travelled faster by horse-drawn Russian *tarantass* along better roads, a further seven hundred miles to the Soviet border and the Trans Siberian railway.

They reached England in October 1926 and soon found themselves famous. The courage and endurance of those three women, aged fifty-nine, fifty-seven and fifty, caught the imagination of the nation. Mildred proved an excellent speaker, whether at missionary meetings or to learned societies, and their book, *Through Jade Gate and Central Asia*, became a best seller: it went into twelve editions.

They returned to Suchow eighteen months later in the summer of 1928. Gwa Gwa came round quickly, but the present of cloth they had brought her was promptly seized and sold by her foster mother.

They decided to adopt Gwa Gwa as the only way to help. They bought her for a trifle and changed her name from Little Lonely to *Ai Lien*, meaning "Love Bond"; but because Ai Lien was a difficult name to lip read they always called her Topsy. When they went on their next long journey within the vast Gobi Desert, lasting nearly a year, Topsy went too.

The political scene was now darker. The Muslim Turkus were rising in Sinkiang, while in Kansu and the Gobi a youthful war lord, Ma Chung Ying, known as the Baby General, had taken arms against the weak Chinese government and was laying the province waste. As they travelled the Trio would find a once flourishing oasis town almost destroyed and the survivors starving. They passed grisly scenes of recent battles. At one place they were briefly arrested by soldiers or brigands (the distinction was slight), and though treated courteously were harrowed by the sight of flogged conscripts, whose festering wounds from the lash they washed and dressed.

They reached the extensive Tunhwang oasis. While they were there it was captured by one of Ma's armies and the women were forbidden to leave. For eight months they were virtually prisoners, though able to move freely within the oasis area, doing what they could to relieve the misery of the inhabitants as boys were conscripted, farms and grain looted until famine reduced even rich merchants to beggary. Typhus swept the oasis. "Dogs and wolves had a good time outside the north gate," wrote Mildred, "for by ancient custom the bodies of all who died in the roadways were wrapped in matting and buried there in shallow graves."

Then General Ma was wounded and Mildred was ordered to proceed to his capital, Ansi, four hard days' journey across the desert, to dress his wounds. The Trio refused to be separated or to leave Topsy behind. Singing *Guide Me O Thou Great Jehovah*, as they always did before each day's journey, they set out on a cold November morning with a party of prisoners.

When they stood in the presence of the famous general, "We had expected to meet a dashing young warrior; we found a slim youth. There was a smiling, cruel sensuousness about him, and a shallow flippancy, yet he was reported to be an excellent horseman and a skilled athlete." The Baby General, so callous in sending men to death or torture, was a coward when confronted with iodine, but under Mildred's care his wounds healed rapidly.

As she prepared the dressings at a side table he would be enjoying his power. A frightened peasant would fall on his knees before Ma: "Spare my son's life, Your Excellency!"

"Why should I spare his life?" sneered Ma, twirling a hunting knife but never looking at the man.

"He is my only son, Your Excellency."

"The boy is disobedient and I have ordered the disobedient to be shot!"

"I promise he will never do it again, Excellency."

"He has done it once and that is enough. I do not change my mind. You may go." And the bodyguards hustled the man away before the General could fly into a rage and order floggings right and left.

When Ma was healed the Trio wanted to return to Tunhwang, and after much delay he consented. At their last audience Mildred looked the General straight in the eye. She produced a New Testament and a copy of the Ten Commandments, and solemnly bade him care for his soul. He took the books and stood motionless, listening, while the bodyguards marvelled at Mildred's courage. Without a word he saluted them and they retired.

Back at Tunhwang they planned to escape across the Gobi, putting aside every day a small store from the meagre rations of flour and fodder. Early one morning, when most of the town was sleeping off its opium, they drove out of the gate with Topsy, as if to visit a nearby farm. Once out of sight of the guards they changed direction: "We turned our mules' heads towards one of the loneliest of desert roads, known only to local men." They knew they must pass a military post on the edge of the oasis, but to their amazement they learned at the last farm that it was deserted: every soldier had gone on a looting raid. The Trio left the oasis still undetected and travelled hard, lying hidden at night. Once they were caught up by a patrol of Ma's men, who had noticed the cart ruts; but the Trio guessed that the soldiers were illiterate and foxed them by brandishing the majestic sealed passports of the Chinese government which Ma was fighting.

Mildred, who was often inclined to worry and doubt, wondered if they had done right to escape, but when a band of Muslim thieves had let them pass unscathed, and they had not been attacked by wolves, and had galloped through streams without the axle breaking, and had survived the nervous horrors of burned out towns and wayside skeletons, even Mildred became sure, as she lay awake exhausted under the stars, that "He, watching over Israel, slumbers not nor sleeps".

They reached the safety of an oasis in the hot but lush Turfan Depression. The town was in government hands and they could relax. Mildred went to the stables of the inn to see that Molly and the other mule were being looked after. She did not return. Eva went to look and found her unconscious in the filth, bleeding from a vicious kick on the head by a tired donkey.

With the help of a kindly Chinese gardener who welcomed them to the shade of his mulberry trees beside running water, they slowly nursed her back to health.

.   .   .   .   .

"There is no denying that signs of wear and tear are evident, so we prefer to travel without a mirror!" But they added: "The meaning and reality of Christ have become intense. He is Saviour, Guardian, Friend – way and end. We have lacked nothing."

They finally left the Gobi when all missionaries were orderd out of the North–West in 1936 at a time of political disturbance. By then they had seen many Christian groups flourish, though sometimes persecuted; groups which were the foundation of the church in Kansu which survived the reign of Mao and all that happened after.

The Trio, with Topsy, devoted the rest of their lives to the Bible Society, which had been their strong ally throughout, and to lecturing and writing.

Their base was a little cottage near Shaftesbury in Dorset and there, when a schoolboy, I had tea with them and Topsy, the only subjects of these sketches that I ever met.

12
Victims of the Long March

John and Betty Sram
1916–1934 1917–1934

It was a prosaic, peaceful world, though locally there
had been disturbances from bandits and Communists.
America was immersed in the New Deal, England
with preparations for the Silver Jubilee of King
George V. Hitler was not yet a menace, and the
League of Nations still had respect. War, bloodshed
and murder were not much in mind, and as for new
names on the roll of Christian martyrs, the possibility,
in October 1934, seemed so remote as to be almost
absurd.

A young American and a middle-aged Englishman
were closeted with the district magistrate of Tsingteh,
Anhwei province, a decayed little town a few hundred
miles from Nanking. The American and the Englishman were missionaries of the China Inland Mission.

Martyrdom was far from the thoughts of John
Stam, the young American, as he listened to his
senior colleague asking the magistrate whether it
would be safe for John to bring his wife and their
month-old baby to live in Tsingteh. The magistrate
admitted that there had been banditry, for the
countryside was half-starving, but he was soothing

in his protestations of security.

John Stam remarked that they did not want to meet the Communists, who had been passing through the next province during their famous "long march" after defeat in South China.

"Oh, no, no!" the magistrate exclaimed. "There is no danger of Communists here. As far as that is concerned, you may come at once and bring your family. I will guarantee your safety, and if there should be any trouble you can come to my *yamen*."

A month later John and Betty Stam and the baby, Helen Priscilla, made their home in the disused Tsingteh mission compound in the middle of the town, with a background of distant mountains.

John Stam was twenty-eight, a tall athletic New Yorker whose Dutch extraction showed in his fair hair and blue eyes. Betty, a year younger, had been born in China, daughter of an American missionary doctor. They had met at Moody Bible Institute in Chicago. Both were unusual personalities. Betty, for instance, could write verse of distinction. And John, in Chicago, had deliberately tested his faith, like the young Hudson Taylor at Hull eighty years earlier, by concealing his financial needs from his family and friends and depending only on God in prayer.

Betty had served her first year in China before John reached Shanghai. On 25th October 1933, a year to the day before the meeting with the magistrate, they had been married at Betty's home in North China. Two happy, unpretentious missionaries at the start of a lifetime of service, they were unreservedly dedicated to their call but aware of how much they had to learn, ready for the hardships and setbacks of

Christian work in a foreign land, yet young enough to extract enjoyment from any situation. Their aim was simple: to "talk about Him to everybody, and live so closely with Him and in Him, that others may see that there really is such a person as Jesus."

Tsingteh was their first station on their own away from seniors. The opening ten days were much like any other missionary's introduction to a new location in China, with inquisitive Chinese crowding around so that privacy was impossible. The Stams visited the few Christians, preached in the little chapel, administered famine relief, and spoke on the streets to the chattering, restless press of peasants, soldiers, and townsfolk.

Early on the eleventh morning, 6th December 1934, Betty Stam was bathing the baby when a man ran in at the door. Out of breath and urging them to hurry, he panted that the magistrate had sent him to warn that the Communists, whom everybody had thought to be beyond the mountains, were advancing on the city after a surprise flank march behind the government army.

John at once sent for coolies and chairs, intending to join the stream of refugees who were hurrying down the street to escape to the safety of the hills. Before the Stams had put together their few necessities, a distant burst of firing proved that the battle had reached the town, where the Communists quickly scaled the walls and opened the gates. As the chair-coolies loped into the courtyard the Stams heard that the magistrate had fled. They bolted the door, realizing that escape was now impossible. Scattered shots, the crackle of flames, and the

screams of townsfolk in the street made this all too
obvious.

John told the servants to kneel. He began to
lead in prayer, but the prayer was interrupted by
a thundering knock on the door. Red soldiers demanded admittance. John spoke to them courteously.
Betty, as calm as if the soldiers were inquirers for
the faith, offered them tea and cakes. These were
brusquely refused. John was tightly bound and taken
across to the communist headquarters. Betty and the
baby were brought in later.

John and Betty stood together, bound, yet serene
despite the suddenness of the catastrophe. The Stams
had been allowed none of the mental or spiritual
preparation which would have been theirs had these
events occurred thirty years earlier, when the mar-
tyrdoms of the Boxer Rising were fresh in people's
memory; or thirty years later, when the witness of
Paul Carlson and the Congo martyrs rang round the
world. The Stams faced death unwarned but their
captors saw no trace of fear.

The Communists discussed the Americans' fate in
their hearing. They were imperialists and should
be liquidated. Moreover, the Communists detested
Christians. To make an example of two Christian
leaders should strike terror into the hearts of the
rest. The Reds had no compunction about murdering
Americans, for the affair would merely increase the
embarrassment of Chiang Kai-shek's government in
Nanking.

The one difficulty was what to do with the baby.
Betty heard them say that it had best be spitted on a
bayonet in front of its parents.

A bystander, an old farmer, protested: "The baby has done nothing worthy of death!"

"Then it's your life for hers!" said the Red leader.

The Stams had never seen him before, and certainly had no claim on him, but their serenity and courage had gripped him. "I am willing", he said.

A moment later the man's severed head rolled across the floor.

The Communists abandoned Tsingteh, sacked and burning, and marched their prisoners to a town named Miaosheo. The looting and terror resumed while the Stams were left under guard in the post-master's shop. The Stams had lived in Miaosheo and the postmaster knew them by sight.

"Where are you going?", he asked.

"We do not know where *they* are going," replied John, "but we are going to heaven."

That night the Stams were locked with their guards in an inner room of a deserted mansion. John was tied to a bedpost, but Betty was left free with the baby.

Next morning they were ordered to leave the baby and to strip off their outer garments and shoes – though John managed to give Betty his socks. Then they were both bound tightly and led down the street while the Communists yelled ridicule and shouted to the townsfolk, many of whom had heard the Stams preach here in happier days, to come and see these Christians die. On a little hill outside the town they came to a clump of pines. A Communist began to harangue the trembling crowd, pouring scorn and blasphemies on all that the Stams held dear.

He was in full tilt when a man stepped boldly forward.

The Stams recognized him as Mr Chang the medicine-seller, a nominal Christian who was known as "rather unwilling to witness for the true and living God". This once weak disciple fell on his knees and boldly pleaded for their lives. The Communists pushed him away. He persisted.

"Are you a Christian then?", they said.

Chang knew what his fate could be. "Yes", he replied.

He was dragged away to be butchered, and now it was John Stam's turn to intercede, for Chang. For reply John was ordered to kneel. People in that crowd said afterwards there was a "look of joy on his face".

The Chinese executioner, in time-honoured style, held the sword level with both hands, whirled round and round to gather momentum, and struck. Betty was seen to quiver for a moment, then she fell unconscious across the body. A few moments later her head too was on the ground and the Reds were driving the crowd away.

Two days afterwards, when the Communists had left to spread their trail of bloodshed and fire further across the province, an evangelist of Miaosheo named Lo, whose leadership hitherto had been indifferent returned with other refugees. Lo had heard rumours of the murder but found difficulty in obtaining facts because no one dared side with the Christians for fear lest the Reds return.

Following clues, he discovered the Stam baby, hungry but warm and alive in her zip-fastened sleeping bag in an abandoned house. He left her in the care of his wife.

Next he climbed the hillside where the headless bodies still lay, stiff and grotesque. He went back to the town and brought coffins, followed now by a crowd made braver through his courage. Lo and two other Christians, a woman and her son, placed the bodies in the coffins and bowed their heads in prayer. This formerly unsatisfactory half-hearted evangelist then turned to the crowd and told them that the Stams lived "in the presence of their heavenly Father. They came to China and to Miaosheo, not for themselves but for you, to tell you about the great love of God that you might believe in the Lord Jesus and be eternally saved. You have heard their message. Remember it is true. Their death proves it so. Do not forget what they told you – repent, and believe the Gospel."

Many of the crowd were weeping as Lo set out on a hundred-mile escape through the Communist-held territory, with his wife, to bring little Helen Stam to the nearest missionaries.

In the years that followed, many millions of men and women throughout the world were to die by violence. But John and Betty were martyred in time of peace, when such an event seemed incredible, and they died because of their faith. As always, the blood of martyrs was the seed of the Church. The shock of their death turned timid Evangelist Lo into a courageous preacher. The story of their steadfastness prepared their fellow missionaries in China for the testing times of the Sino-Japanese and Pacific wars.

The impact on the student world was enormous, for the Stams had been fresh from college. One of those who gave herself for missionary service as a direct result of reading about the Stams was an American girl who became Mrs Hector McMillan. Thirty years later she escaped death by inches in the Congo, a few moments before her husband became one of the Stanleyville martyrs. As Ione McMillan had pledged herself to fill the gap in the missionary ranks left by the Stams, so her son, young Kenneth McMillan, as he lay wounded near the body of his father, pledged himself to return as a missionary to speak of Christ's love to the murderers.

Isles of the Southern Sea

13
Cannibal Easter

James Chalmers 1841–1901

A mob of howling, naked, war-painted savages swarmed around a native house above the sandy foreshore of a river mouth in unexplored New Guinea on an afternoon in December 1877. Inside the house a white woman sat sewing. The movement of her fingers gave no indication of her fervent but not quite agitated inward praying. Near her crouched three Polynesian teachers and their wives. Strong Christians from distant South Sea islands, they were struggling now with the uncomfortable conviction that their missionary service was about to end summarily in a cooking pot.

Down on the shore the white woman's husband had been signaling to his lugger for some stores when he heard the commotion behind. James Chalmers, a strongly built Scotsman of thirty-six, with bushy black beard, ran up to the native house, pushed his way through a ring of cannibals, and climbed the platform.

"One evil-looking fellow wearing a human jawbone and carrying a heavy stone club rushed towards me as if to strike", Chalmers wrote later. "Looking him steadily in the face our eyes met, and I demanded

in loud, angry tones what he wanted." By signs and
unintelligible noises the cannibal demanded tomahawks, knives, iron and beads, adding "that if they
were not given they were going to kill us."

"You may kill us," shouted the white man, "but
never a thing will you get from us." His tones
conveyed the intensity of his displeasure to men
whose language he had not yet had time to learn.

A Polynesian teacher approached. "Tamate," he
implored the white man, using Chalmers' South Seas
name and speaking in the language of Rarotonga,
the island which they had all left to evangelize New
Guinea, "please give him a little something or we will
all be murdered!"

"No", Tamate replied. "Can't you see that if I
give them something because they threaten us, every
group in the district will try the same trick. When
there's nothing left they will murder us. Let them
murder us now and be done with it!"

One of the cannibals, a friendly man from the house
where the missionaries had lived since their landing
three days earlier, told Tamate by signs that the
violent savages came from across the river. He had
better give them something to get rid of them.

Tamate, ignoring the angry roars and brandished
clubs, smiled at him but shook his head. He would
not give anything to armed men. "We have never
carried arms and have lived among you as friends."
The friendly cannibal harangued the crowd – which
then retired to consider the situation. Thus the
immediate danger was past. A deputation came
forward to repeat the request, and again met refusal.
Then they dispersed.

Next day their chief came, unarmed and unpainted, to say "Sorry!" Tamate grinned happily at him, took him into the house and gave him a present. Jeanie Chalmers, still sewing, prayed that the cannibal would soon receive the Best Gift of all.

James and Jeanie Chalmers had served some ten years in the settled island of Rarotonga before pioneering in New Guinea. James Chalmers, "Tamate", was the son of a stonemason in the western highlands of Scotland, where he had been thoroughly grounded in the deep if stern religious convictions of an unbending Calvinism. He had even determined as a boy to be a missionary to cannibals, but subsequently decided that he was not among God's elect. Missionary ambition faded in favour of allowing full play to an irrepressible sense of fun. His practical jokes and youthful escapades sent shudders through the staid little fishing port of Inveraray, nestling beside the great castle of the Duke of Argyll.

When Chalmers was eighteen, during the revival of 1859, two evangelists were invited to Inveraray. Chalmers attended a meeting in a loft during a heavy rainstorm, and there became aware of the truth of Christ, through the verse from Revelation, "Let him that is athirst come. And whosoever will, let him take the water of life freely."

During training in England he showed himself more than ever a leader – in student pranks as well as in evangelism. A young man of strength, high spirits, humour and intense dedication, he "used to pray for help as if he were at his mother's knee, and to preach as though he were sure of the message he had then to deliver."

His arrival on the mission field was, characteristically though unintentionally, unconventional. The ship was wrecked on a reef in Samoa, and James and Jeanie chartered the brig of a local white pirate whom Chalmers temporarily tamed!

"Tamate", as he was named by the South Sea islanders, had hoped to pioneer at once, but the leaders of the London Missionary Society kept him nearly ten years in an island already evangelized. At last, with a group of his own Rarotongans, he was allowed to adventure into New Guinea. Only six years earlier a small group of missionaries had become the earliest white settlers in a land where strangers lived in hourly expectation of being clubbed, cooked, and eaten. (A friendly native tried to present Jeanie with a portion of oven-fresh human breast.)

After that first landing, which had so nearly ended in death, Chalmers placed a chain of Polynesian teacher-evangelists along the southern coast of Papua New Guinea. In each place he made the first, dangerous contact and stayed until the Papuans were reasonably friendly. He was a man whom they immediately respected and soon loved – tall, strong, impulsive, generous, quick-tempered but quick to laugh. He had no trace of a white man's pomposity, yet his character conveyed such authority that no native liked to cross him. He was fearless, again and again taking his life in his hands. And he brimmed over with a genuine, utterly unsentimental love, knowing that even the most depraved and cruel could be transformed by the love and Spirit of Christ.

Tamate's methods were always unconventional. He had no horror of using tobacco or tomahawks as currency. Once he caused merriment in the City of London by cabling: "Send one gross tomahawks, one gross butcher knives. Going east try make friends between tribes." He was a great explorer, but always as a means of spreading the Gospel. He found a people sunk in degradation, violence and fear. Chalmers knew that his hard and dangerous labour was worthwhile because in time "all these evils would yield to the Gospel. God is Love, seen in Christ: this was the life word we brought them. The Gospel was working its way in bush-clearing, fencing, planting, housebuilding; through fun, play, feasting, travelling, joking, laughing, and along the ordinary experience of everyday life."

Tamate lived Christ. He preached Christ as the one who could save to the uttermost those who came to Him. And he rejoiced at last to hear a young Papuan, so recently a cannibal, say to his fellow tribesmen, "The time has come to be up and doing. Foreigners have brought us the Gospel; many have died of fever, several have been speared and tomahawked. Now let us carry the Gospel to other districts and if we die, it is well: we die in Christ. If we are murdered, it is well: it is in carrying His name and love, and will be for Him. Let us do it!"

For twenty-three years Tamate and his Polynesians and Papuans evangelized, pacified, and civilized great stretches of the New Guinea coastland, and up into the nearer mountains as far as they could go. While her husband pioneered, Jeanie stayed bravely in their first cannibal village in order to show the trust that always breeds trust, but eventually the climate drove her to Australia where she died. After nine lonely

years Tamate married again. It was soon after this
that Robert Louis Stevenson, then living in Polynesia,
described him in letters home as "a man nobody can
see and not love. . . . A big, stout, wildish-looking
man, iron grey, with big bold black eyes and a deep
furrow down each cheek. . . . With no humbug,
plenty of courage, and the love of adventure. . . .
He has plenty of faults like the rest of us but he's
as big as a church."

All this time Tamate had no permanent white
helper. "We need help," he wrote home, "missionaries willing to live among the savages, men
and women who will joyfully endure the hardship
of the climate for Christ's sake." When at length he
heard that someone was appointed he commented,
"I hope he is a good all-around man without namby-
pambyism, ready for all sorts of roughing it." And in
Oliver Tomkins he found a man after his own heart.

Within weeks of Tomkins' arrival Chalmers' second
wife fell ill. In the long period of nursing her before
she died, the young recruit became as a dear son to the
veteran. After the burial they spent months touring
the settled stations which Tomkins would supervise.
Then they set off for the notorious Aird River delta
where Tamate planned to pioneer, along coasts which
no missionary had penetrated, where Christ had "not
been named". He had reconnoitred the area, knew
"the savages there are splendid fellows. If only
I can get hold of them they will make splendid
missionaries."

As Tamate and Tomkins, with their party consist-
ing of a Polynesian teacher, a Papuan Christian chief
and ten embryo Papuan missionaries, approached

Goaribari Island, it happened that the inhabitants of a village named Dopina had just completed a new *dubu* or communal house for fighting men. Built of sago-palm timber, a *dubu* was not ready for use without human sacrifice. The next strangers to the island would serve for the consecration and the feast.

When the mission lugger rounded the headland, the men of the village at once paddled out and swarmed aboard. Tamate was used to such invasions, the normal prelude to his entry into a new village.

It was Easter Sunday evening, 7th April 1901. As the sun dropped swiftly to the brief tropical dusk, Tamate promised to visit the village in peace. He tried in vain to persuade the armed men to leave the vessel. To draw them off he said he would go ashore at once in the whale boat for half an hour and be back for supper. Tomkins said he would go too. They set off, crewed by the ten mission boys and the chief.

Tamate knew nothing about the new *dubu*, but he was ready as always "to die for the name of the Lord Jesus". Young Tomkins had no fear of death either.

The boat reached shore. While the chief and most of the mission boys stayed on guard, the two missionaries accepted the villagers' pressing invitation to enter the *dubu* for refreshment. They sat down on the floor, Tamate cracking jokes with his new neighbours and, as always, praying in his heart to the Companion whose Easter message he brought. All around him in the fading light were piles of human skulls at the feet of coarse wooden images.

Two swift blows from behind by stone clubs. Two cassowary-bone daggers swiftly plunged into the gullets of the white men. While the mission boys were set upon and murdered, the heads of Tamate and Tomkins were severed from their bodies. They were stripped, deftly cut into joints and passed to the women to be cooked, mixed with sago.

To the Western world, when the news came, the Easter massacre seemed a foul and obscene ending to two lives of goodwill – one famous and honoured, one young and promising. To the people of the village the cannibal feast was the prelude to their eventual discovery of Christ.

To Tamate and Tomkins it was a painless transition from the Easter Faith to the Easter Presence.

14
Tuan Change

Ernest Presswood
1908–1946

On the Sarawak coast in East Malaysia a missionary tapped excitedly at the typewriter as she compiled an information sheet datelined 1968: "Reports have been coming through of a great stirring among the churches of Indonesian Borneo. . . . Several Christians have had visions from the Lord which they have been told to proclaim to their people, and as a result hundreds have repented from sin and turned to the Lord. The spiritual stirring is influencing Murut and Kelabit churches on the Sarawak border."

She glanced across the airstrip to the Bible School. They were just clearing up after the half yearly conference which two hundred indigenous pastors and leaders had attended. Some had walked eight days through the jungle, others had come by mission plane or river boat, and they represented an expanding, missionary-hearted church of many tribes in the mountains and jungles of former British Borneo.

It all went back to the pioneering of one forgotten North American, William Ernest Presswood who, because he died young a few months after the end of World War II and lies buried in Borneo, has been largely forgotten except by those who loved him. But his name is legendary among the natives of the interior: they call him Tuan Change – because so many were changed from a particularly evil darkness into the light of Christ.

Ernie Presswood was born in the prairies of Canada in 1908, son of English immigrants. In a Sunday school class which could boast of eleven who later were ministers or missionaries, he gave his heart to Christ, yet it was not until the Presswoods returned to England briefly in the early 1920s, and he heard Gypsy Smith, that he dedicated himself for service. His father next bought a meat and grocery store in Toronto, where Ernie trained as a motor mechanic. Then, after Prairie Bible School and the missionary institute at Nyack, New York, he joined the Christian and Missionary Alliance in the Netherlands East Indies during 1930.

About eighteen months later a most extraordinary rumour passed around the Murut or Dayak natives for up-country in the interior. As it was told to me in Borneo long after, by a Murut named Panai Raub, "We were clearing the undergrowth for the new season's farming when we heard of a wonderful white man they called Tuan Change because he changed wicked natives and said they could have a new life. He was on an island off the coast." They wanted to go down but were afraid of venturing where Malays, Chinese, and whites lived.

The Muruts, a large tribe scattered across the mountains of the British-Dutch border, were steeped in spirit-worship to such an extent that planting would be endlessly delayed for lack of an omen, or the half-grown paddy abandoned as the result of another. They turned most of the harvest into intoxicating ricebeer, sapped their tribal stamina by sexual malpractices, and frequently went head-hunting. They lived naked except for loin-cloths.

"When I heard," Panai Raub continued, "way up in the hills in the midst of all that drinking and fear of the spirits, about change and new life, I just could not sleep for desire. Two months later when we were felling the big timber we heard that Tuan Change was downstream. We all went to meet him, taking our sick."

They found Presswood at Long Berang, a place above fearsome rapids which had needed consider-able courage for a lone Westerner to negotiate, even with skilled boatmen. A huge crowd of Muruts, heads bowed, squatted round Presswood who was standing with eyes closed, arms outstretched to the sky.

"What is this?", thought Panai Raub. "What are they doing?"

After praying, Tuan Change unfolded some pic-tures, and preached in Malay with one of the few educated Muruts to interpret. Panai Raub was right in front.

"I could hear every word. Some of the others could not. He preached on the Resurrection, with amazing effect on the crowd. Right from the beginning it hit me. I was just drinking it in. When I first heard the Word I believed."

This was in September 1932. Next day Tuan Change left them and walked far over rugged jungle trails in great heat until forced back to the coast with a foot ulcerated by leech bites. He wrote home: "What a time I have had. Physically it has been a hard one but the results have been *glorious*. I think around six hundred Dayaks were reached with the message."

Ernie Presswood was now nearly twenty-five. He was a true pioneer, willing to forgo the good things he enjoyed. He pushed himself relentlessly. "His middle name could have been 'hurry'", writes one who knew him well. "It was always praying, reading, teaching, counselling, studying, and the little notebook always at hand." He seemed austere, not quick to laugh though with a genuine sense of humour. He was a perfectionist and could be hard on those who had openly acknowledged Christ yet failed Him, when Presswood would hide the compassion which ran strong within. His was a character that could be appreciated and admired by Muruts, who seemed so feckless then, yet subsequently disclosed the same characteristics of uncompromising dedication.

Presswood was kept at the coast by his bad foot until 1934 when he paid a second visit to Long Berang. "I have been here two weeks, twice as long as I expected, the interest has been so great. From early morning till late at night I have been kept busy with scarcely a break. Pray much for me for the strain is very great. Thus far I have baptized a hundred and thirty and I expect there will be at least twice as many more." After a third, longer visit he returned to America, married Laura Harmon from Pennsylvania, and in May 1937 they settled in Long Berang, having taken twenty nine days negotiating the rapids.

That Christmas there was a great baptism at Long Berang; one of those baptized was Panai Raub. The following April, Presswood could write of a "morning service at which the Spirit of God was manifest in a very real way. Waves of praise swept over us as we looked into the faces of these happy Christians."

A few days later, when the Presswoods were still the only whites upriver, Laura had a miscarriage. Complications developed. There was nothing Ernie could do but see her die, and bury her in a coffin made with his own hands from one of the timbers with which they were building their home. Despite sorrowing natives he felt desperately alone. "Only those who have passed through such a heart-breaking experience can appreciate the distress." Then floods swept down on Long Berang, carrying away much of their precious timber. "Surely the Lord doesn't love me when He treats me thus, I thought: but He answered me so blessedly, 'Whom the Lord loveth He chasteneth and scourgeth every son he receives. . . .' The comfort and blessing that He has already sent upon my soul has strengthened me and given me courage to face the future."

For Borneo, it was already proving a great future, for the revival was spreading right across the border. The Sarawak Muruts had been even worse than the Indonesian. Officials of Rajah Brooke, the English ruler, estimated the whole community except the dogs to be drunk a hundred days in a year. After Tuan Change's first visit to Long Berang rumours of his good words had filtered over the border, and some Sarawak Muruts went to find an Australian missionary, Hudson Southwell, who returned with them in 1933. Several were converted, but Rajah Brooke reckoned the Muruts were irredeemable. He refused Southwell permission to settle, threw a

cordon sanitaire round the whole tribe, and left it to
die out.

Panai Raub and other baptized Muruts determined
to evangelize their cousins. Presswood had not told
them they should. He so preached Christ that converts caught the vision for themselves; long before
it became accepted missionary strategy Presswood
urged that a church should be self-propagating and
self-supporting.

"The first village I came to," Panai Raub says, "just
over the border, a big drinking party was on. I refused
it: 'I do not drink now.' 'Why not?' 'Because I follow
the Lord Jesus Christ.' 'Where did you hear about
Him?' 'From Tuan Change.' 'Does he live near this
Lord Jesus?' They were very pleased and keen to hear.
Even the old people who had been heavily involved in
headhunting and the old worship brought the fetishes
and burned them."

Panai Raub was not yet literate and no Scriptures
had been translated; he preached with the aid of
pictures. On his next visit he found that drinking
had been abandoned. Wherever he went "there was
not one house among the Muruts which did not want
to hear. . . . 'Eternal life. *That's* what we want', they
would say." After he left, a village would choose its
own church leaders from those who showed the gifts
of the Spirit.

Late in 1938 the Rajah of Sarawak heard that
something extraordinary had occurred. He ordered
an expedition of inquiry, led by a government official
and a missionary, who travelled among the Muruts
from 12th December 1938 to 4th February 1939. The
Government official reported that he was not popular

with the Muruts because he smoked, drank whisky, and did not possess a Sankey hymnbook! After that missionaries of the Borneo Evangelical Mission were allowed to settle.

Meanwhile across the border, Presswood undertook even more rigorous climbs to reach mountain villages, and by the time he left for his second furlough late in 1939 the Murut church was growing rapidly.

In America he was married again, to Ruth Brooks of Buffalo, N.Y., who returned with him in May 1940. He was appointed to head the Bible School at Makassar in the Celebes where the Japanese invasion engulfed him. Beaten, starved, forced to do coolie labour, kept in a pig house, he watched his brother missionaries die; even when giving a funeral address in a prison camp he was able to win men to Christ.

On 27th November 1945 the Presswoods returned to Borneo. Ernie discovered the grave of his successor, who had been bayoneted to death after surrendering to prevent reprisals on the natives. When the Presswoods went up-country, they found that the war had divided loyalties, caused disputes and much backsliding, even some rebuilding of spirit altars. "Such things were disheartening to Ernie", writes Ruth. But there were repentances, and much hunger.

Nor need Presswood have feared. The horrors of the Pacific War, the disturbances of the War of Independence, and the checkered growth of Sukarno's Indonesia could not quench so deep a movement of the Spirit. Over the Sarawak border a great forward movement began in the 1950s, with the Muruts as the spearhead bringing the Gospel to other tribes, while the Borneo Evangelical missionaries translated the

Scriptures into the different languages, ran a Bible
School, and set up their own air service.

Ernie Presswood did not live to see it. At Long Berang on that first post-war visit of January 1946, a severe
bout of sickness convinced him, physically weak from
his sufferings as a prisoner, that he must return downstream to the coast at once, several days early, or die.
The river was high but a legend among the Muruts that
natives tried to stop him travelling is disproved by contemporary letters. On Ernie's thirty-eighth birthday
the Presswoods set off, with seven boatmen and another passenger carrying a live pig to sell at the market.

At the first rapid they had to land and crawl among
the leeches through the edge of the undergrowth.
After that the going was easier. "We continued
shooting rapids for several hours and I found it fun",
writes Ruth. At the last and biggest, the boatmen
climbed up the mountain side to reconnoitre and
reported it safe to negotiate, so they floated out past
a big boulder. They were struck by a ten foot wave.
The next capsized them. Ruth could not swim and
Ernie grabbed her. They were carried downstream
three hundred yards, much of it underwater.

They scrambled ashore, safe except for the baggage
which was nearly all lost, and finally reached the coast
after a trying journey in an overloaded motor boat
wedged among prisoners of war.

The drenching seriously affected Presswood's shat-
tered constitution. But he had promised to attend a conference across the bay, and though feeling ill, and Ruth
sick and unable to accompany him, he kept his word.
Pneumonia set in and on 1st February 1946 he died.

His memorial is the vigorous evangelical church in
Borneo.

Hills of the North Rejoice

15
Santa Claus of Labrador

Sir Wilfred Grenfell 1865–1940

One Christmas morning in the early nineteen hundreds the people of a small isolated fishing village in Labrador were gathered outside their doors watching an unusual sight. A sledge was coming towards them across the frozen bay. But instead of the team of husky dogs it was drawn by a reindeer – an animal unknown in Labrador, though closely related to the wild caribou of the forests. The sledge drew nearer and the fishermen and their wives – descendants of the original British settlers – soon saw that the sledge carried their great friend, the Good Samaritan of the Coast, Wilfred Grenfell.

Crowding round him as he unloaded his surgical instruments for an emergency operation, they asked him how and why he had put a stag into harness. "Milk! Milk! Milk!", he replied, at which they blinked, though they knew the doctor's jovial ways. After a little more leg-pulling, he explained that he had introduced a herd of domestic reindeer from Lapland as a substitute for dairy cows, which could not exist on the Coast, thus hoping to provide people with the fresh milk they sorely needed. Some of the stags he was using for transport. Marvelling at the doctor's unending ideas for their assistance, the rugged fisherfolk waited while he performed the surgery for which he had come, and then joined him for a simple Christmas service, lustily singing the old hymns and listening with bowed heads as Grenfell prayed extempore in the most natural, unaffected way.

Grenfell had already done much to transform the lives of the scattered fishing and trapping communities of Labrador. In the snowy wastes of the North he was a veritable embodiment of the Christmas spirit, bringing throughout the year good things for body and soul alike. To him this was no matter for boasting, but just a response to one of his favourite verses from the Psalms, "Teach me to do the thing that pleaseth Thee".

It all traced back to a winter's day in the slums of East London early in 1885. Grenfell, a young medical student in his second year, a keen rowing man and rugby football player, and devoted to the sea and outdoor life, happened to wander into a large tent erected on a piece of derelict ground in dockland, near where he had been sent to attend a case. He found himself in a meeting of Moody and Sankey's second London campaign. "It was so new to me," records Grenfell, "that when a tedious prayer bore began with a long oration, I started to leave. Suddenly the leader, who I learned afterwards was D. L. Moody, called out to the audience, 'Let us sing a hymn while our brother finishes his prayer.' His practicality interested me and I stayed the service out." He left "with a determination either to make religion a real effort to do as I thought Christ would do in my place as a doctor, or frankly abandon it."

For some weeks he hovered; to come out for Christ in the "coarse and evil environment" of the hospital medical school required more pluck than even Wilfred Grenfell possessed. Then he attended a meeting at which the speakers were the Studd brothers – it was a short while before C. T. Studd sailed with the Cambridge Seven. The fact that they were noted athletes made Grenfell hang on their words. "I felt I could listen to them. I could not have listened to a sensuous-looking man, a man who was not a master of his own body." At the end of the service the Studds asked all those who would give their lives to Christ to stand up. There was dead silence and no one stirred. "It seemed a very sensible question to me," wrote Grenfell, "but I was amazed how hard I found it to stand up. At last one boy, out of a hundred or more in sailor rig from a reformatory ship on the Thames, suddenly rose. It seemed to me such a wonderfully courageous act – for I knew perfectly what it would mean to him – that I immediately found myself on my feet."

Grenfell scorned mere theorizing. He had no truck with people who talked pious and never lifted a finger to serve Christ or their fellows. At once he began work among the boys in his neighbourhood, running a Sunday school with such vigour that the staid parson, shocked by his introduction of boxing on weekday evenings, forced him to resign. He therefore joined up with a "ragged school", which with East End boys in the eighteen eighties required as much physical hardihood as spiritual zeal. To this he added

lodging-house work and temperance campaigning in
the worst of the slum saloons. Once the angry topers
made preparations to beat him up and pour whisky
down his throat: "however they greatly overrated
their stock of fitness and equally underrated my good
training, for the scrimmage went all my way in a very
short time."

Grenfell's holidays were always spent sailing, with
his brother and a few friends hiring an old fishing
sr ack in the Irish sea. "One result of these holidays
was that I told my London boys about them, using
one's experiences as illustrations, till suddenly it
struck me that this was shabby Christianity." After
that, he always took some of them with him, and
in subsequent summers he ran camping and boating
holidays on the Welsh coast, with straight-from-the-
shoulder talks on the Christian life to end each day.

From sailing holidays to service on the sea was a
natural move. Shortly after he had qualified as a
doctor and finished his hospital training, his great
friend and teacher, the brilliant surgeon Sir Frederick
Treves, told him that a recently formed mission
(afterwards the Royal National Mission to Deep Sea
Fishermen) was looking for a doctor to help them
among the North Sea herring fleet which stayed at
sea for months at a time. They had "chartered a small
fishing smack, and sent her out among the fishermen
to hold religious services of a simple, unconventional
type, in order to afford the men an alternative to the
grog vessels when fishing was slack." Grenfell joined
at Yarmouth, wondering whether he would be of any
use among such men "far older and tougher and more
experienced than I." But on the wheel of the Mission

ship was engraved "Follow Me and I will make you fishers of men." "That was a real challenge," recalled Grenfell, "and I knew then perfectly well that that was my only chance, anyhow."

Four years later, in 1892, he set out at the Mission's invitation to cross the far north of the Atlantic in a sailing vessel to see if he could help the fishermen of Labrador and North Newfoundland. The coasts would be wild, lonely and cold, though the expedition was only for the few summer months. But the venture seemed no sacrifice to Grenfell. "I have always believed that the Good Samaritan went across the road to the wounded man just because he wanted to", he once remarked. And besides, there was "everything about such a venture as sailing to Labrador to attract my type of mind."

After calling at St Johns they made landfall in Labrador. "A serried rank of range upon range of hills, reaching north and south as far as the eye could see from the masthead, was rising above our horizon behind a very surfeit of islands." At their first harbour they were bombarded with calls for medical help from ships and shore. That evening, when the last patient had left the spotless dispensary on board the mission schooner, Grenfell noticed "a miserable bunch of boards, serving as a boat, with only a dab of tar along its seams lying motionless a little way from us. In it, sitting silent, was a half-clad, brown haired, brown faced figure." After a prolonged stare the man in the boat suddenly said, "Be you a doctor?" "That's what I call myself", replied Grenfell with the twinkle in his eyes which was to become so well known and loved throughout Labrador. "Us hasn't got no money," said the half-clothed settler, "but there's a very sick man is here, if so be you'd come and see him."

Grenfell was led to a small, bare, filthy hovel, crowded with neglected children. "A very sick man was coughing his soul out in the darkness while a pitiably covered woman gave him cold water to sip out of a spoon." The man's case was hopeless, and with his death starvation would be a grim reality for the whole family; government relief was a mockery because of the iniquities of the local trading system. Thus Grenfell was faced with something of the need of Labrador. As he put it, "to pray for the man, and with the family was easy, but scarcely satisfying." Grenfell knew that Christ would not have him leave it at that.

And thus year by year he returned to Labrador, to do what he could for their bodies and souls, and at last made his home on the Coast and stayed the whole year round. Among the bleak headlands and scattered islands washed by roaring seas in summer and gripped by ice in winter, wherever ship or sledge could take him, he carried the love of Christ, not in word only but in deeds. His frank speech laced with the merry yarns that the fisherfolk loved brought him right to their hearts. And they knew that he was as skilful and hardy a sailor as themselves.

He soon found that much of the misery of the Coast was caused by the grip of corrupt traders, aided by an outdated system of commerce. He proposed the creation of co-operative stores. The vested interests of the colony were enraged and made common cause to crush him. Moreover the settlers who stood to gain most were afraid to join and when he persuaded them, "not one shareholder wished to have his name registered, and one and all they were opposed to having the little building labeled as a store – so ingrained was their fear of their suppliers." But despite setbacks and losses, Grenfell's scheme survived, and like the hospitals and dispensaries and schools which he built, helped to make the life of the settlers more tolerable and to open their hearts to the Gospel.

On one voyage his little hospital ship had dropped anchor among a group of islands. "Suddenly a boat bumped our side and a woman climbed over the rail with a bundle under each arm. On my chartroom table she laid the two bundles and proceeded to untie them." They proved to be twin babies, "blind as kittens". The mother had four other children and her husband had been killed in an accident three months earlier. "What ever are you going to do with the babies?", asked Grenfell. "Give them to you, Doctor."

When the ship was under way again, in a choppy sea, the babies howled so loudly that the helmsman "stuck his head into the chartroom, which was directly behind the wheelhouse." "What are you going to do with those, sir?", he asked. "Shh," replied Grenfell, "they're blind and quite useless. When we get outside, we'll drop them over the rail." "He stared at me for a second," records Grenfell, "before he turned back to the wheel. A few minutes later in popped his head again. 'Excuse my being so bold, but don't throw them over the side. We've got eight of our own, but I guess my wife'll find a place for those two.'" Grenfell laughingly told him that he had already begun to form a collection of derelict children at his base at St Anthony's, to which these would be added.

And thus the work grew. As the years passed, Grenfell's fame spread across North America and in Britain, and funds and volunteers flowed to his aid. After the First World War, in an age which tended to divorce social welfare from spirituality and in which many of the younger generation were ashamed of open profession of faith, Grenfell stood as a virile example of practical Christian love which counts service a privilege and spices it with humour and a refusal to be beaten. "The King Himself", he once wrote, "cannot win His battle without us, He having entrusted us with the task, ensuring victory if we 'are bound to Him'."

Grenfell was often near death as he made his way through ice and storms on sea and land. At Easter 1908, at the age of forty-three, he was caught with his team of huskies on a pan of ice during a sudden thaw and was rapidly drifting out to sea, to drown, or die by cold and starvation if the ice-pan held out. "My own faith in the mystery of immortality is so untroubled that it now seemed almost natural to be passing the portal of death from an ice-pan. Quite unbidden the words of the old hymn kept running through my head, 'Oh, help me from my heart to say, Thy will be done'."

He was rescued just in time. A full span of life was given him, for the good of Labrador and the glory of Christ; and he died in 1940 at the age of seventy-five, after only five years' retirement away from his beloved Coast.

16
Lord Apostol

Lord Radstock 1833–1913

Colonel Paschkov, wealthy darling of St Petersburg society, lolled back in his sumptuous, elegant carriage as it took him swiftly from the palace of his Sovereign and personal friend, Alexander II, Tsar of all the Russias, to a soirée given by a Grand Duchess, a member of the Imperial Family. He thought with satisfaction of his popularity, of his vast estates in the Urals, where his thousands of toiling peasants provided him the wherewithal to live in the extravagant luxury to which he had been bred.

At the Grand Duchess's, gilded doors swung noiselessly open and footmen bowed as the Colonel, resplendent in his Guards' uniform, walked with nonchalant hauteur towards the red-carpeted staircase. The major-domo at the entrance to the great ballroom did not announce him, but respectfully murmured that the guests of her Imperial Highness were already seated. Surprised, Paschkov looked across the long room with its Chinese silks and priceless works of art, and saw a circle of fashionably dressed men and women, most of whom he knew, sitting listening to a plainly dressed gentleman with an English face who stood close to the vast fireplace, talking quietly but earnestly in French, the normal language of the Russian nobility.

Intrigued, Paschkov took a seat and listened. "This same Jesus," the Englishman was saying, and the words seemed strangely out of place in such surroundings, "who sought the fallen woman of Samaria, and Saul of Tarsus, is alive still, the Son of Man, 'who came to seek and to save that which was lost'." Soon the theme changed, and without raising his voice the speaker was castigating the selfish luxury and idleness of his hearers; and his bluntness shook Colonel Paschkov, who had never realized before how empty and self-centred life had been. Then the theme changed again, passing from the certainty of judgement to the wonder of a Saviour who died on the cross. Despite himself, Paschkov was stirred to the depths. This was so different from the contemporary Orthodox Church, with the "insipidity of its traditional bakemeats served by the official clergy in their heavy plates of gold"; it was personal and alive.

As the address closed Paschkov urgently asked his neighbour, a Prince (the highest rank below the Imperial Family) who the man was. "An English milord," the Prince whispered back, "Lord Radstock. The Grand Duchess met him in Paris. She's been a different woman since." That night, kneeling beside Lord Radstock, a Bible open between them, Paschkov gave his life to Christ. . . .

.   .   .   .   .

It was a few months later in this season of 1873–4.

The Minister of the Interior, the clever and cynical Count Brobrinsky, was annoyed. His wife had got herself mixed up with this ridiculous "drawing-room revival" and had just told him that the cause of all the trouble was coming to dinner. Brobrinsky, who had been reading the latest novel, a brilliant skit called *Lord Apostol* which neatly took off the English milord and his absurd converts, had no wish to meet him, but to be absent would be insulting. At dinner, as course after course was handed round on gold plate, Brobrinsky listened with half-amused tolerance as Radstock, who appeared to have no idea as to what subjects were taboo at table, discoursed on the Epistle to the Romans. The Count was frankly agnostic, though to satisfy a vow he had once made when he had believed himself dying he used to say a prayer each day to the Unknown God.

Brobrinsky was certain he could refute all Radstock's statements – the fact of Christ, His resurrection and the possibility of personal faith. When the dessert came, he excused himself, went into his study, and wrote a long refutation which so pleased him that he sent it to be printed. But the eyes and the quiet conviction of the "Lord Apostol", and his sense of the reality of Christ, haunted Brobrinsky. When the manuscript returned and he began to read it, something snapped. As with a flash of light, "I found that Jesus was the key, the beginning and the end of all." He fell on his knees, Cabinet Minister though he was; the Unknown God had revealed Himself. . . .

.   .   .   .   .

Young Princess Catherine Galitzine one day that
same year went round in her sleigh through the
winter streets to see a newly married friend, Princess
Lieven. Both were devout, their emotional natures
drinking in the ritual and stately ceremonial of the
Russian Orthodox Church. The quarterly reception
of the Communion had just taken place, and religion
filled Princess Catherine's heart. Her one distress was
that the glorious feelings would so soon evaporate,
and she must labour on until grace could once more
be received at the next Communion.

As she ran lightly up the wide staircase of the
palace, the boudoir door opened and Princess Lieven,
in her rich brocaded day dress, hurried down to meet
her. Lord Radstock had come to call. The two girls
began to tell him breathlessly of the happiness the
Communion had brought.

"Would you like to possess it for ever?", he asked.

"Impossible", they said.

"And thereupon," Princess Catherine recalled in
her old age, "commenced the Message of Grace
offered us, without the least pressure on our most
precious feelings. Henceforth all the addresses, the
meetings to which we hastened, became as seeds
which the Lord brought to life. At length, one day,
in the American Chapel, after a most blessed address
when the never-to-be-forgotten hymn, "I do believe,
I will believe that Jesus died *for me*", was sung, I
remained for a special conversation – and there we
were both on our knees before *my own Saviour for
ever*". . . .

.   .   .   .   .   .

"Who is Lord Radstock?" – the question was heard
continually as he visited and revisited St Petersburg
and Moscow. Wealthy guardsmen such as Paschkov
threw open their palaces to reach the poorest with
the Gospel; Brobrinsky set himself to win the great
novelist Tolstoy; counts and princes began to treat
their peasants as human beings; and great estates
became centres of evangelism.

He had been born in 1833, the son of an Admiral
who after his retirement had spent many years in
Christian work. By the time he inherited the title
in 1857 Lord Radstock had become a Christian
through the influence of his mother, and in intervals
of soldiering with the newly raised Volunteers, and
absorption in music and literature, he and his young
wife, a famous beauty, had given select Bible Readings in their house in Bryanston Square.

Revival was moving across England in 1859, and
for Lord and Lady Radstock it brought a call to
deliberate service among their own class. Screwing
up his courage, Radstock began to give out tracts,
with a polite lifting of his top hat, at the daily
parades of wealth and fashion in Hyde Park, when
all the world sauntered or rode or sat in gleaming
carriages, to exchange the gossip of Mayfair and
Belgravia. Radstock's tracts, and his invitations to
gospel addresses in the Bryanston Square drawing
room and his Hampshire seat, disgusted his rich titled
contemporaries, secure in their regular churchgoing
and the respectability which too often camouflaged a
carefully hidden immorality.

Despite a life transformed here and there, it

seemed, as so often before, that a man could not reach his own sort, and Radstock turned to the poor who were never far from the streets of fashion in Victorian England. He built them mission halls and refuge centres, and could often be found preaching in the East End of London. As the revival spread in the sixties he became an evangelist who filled halls in watering places and inland towns, moving from mission to mission. In 1867 he was invited to a conference of the Evangelical Alliance in Holland; and the severe, sober, rigidly correct Dutch Calvinist nobility discovered that God could use him to bring them warm personal faith.

After Holland Lord Radstock went to Paris, brilliant capital of the Second Empire, where the ladies of the court in their huge crinolines danced and flirted, oblivious of coming disaster. All the aristocracy of Europe flocked to Paris, and it was among visiting Russians that Radstock found himself most used. His energy was inexhaustible, and he was forever thinking up fresh schemes of evangelization. His impetuousness and bluntness would attract some and alienate others, but those who knew him well were shamed by an unwavering devotion and constancy, by his prayer life, and by his tact in personal dealings, abrupt though he might be in his addresses.

Above all Lord Radstock had that indefinable touch of a man who has learned the secret of steady abiding in Christ. He seemed never to lose contact, however busy the day, and thus had an uncanny knack of being in the right place at the right time, even when a minute or two made all the difference. What others might call coincidences were continually occurring, and it was in this way that he met the Grand Duchess, who had previously refused categorically to be introduced to such a man. But she happened to arrive, uninvited, to spend an evening with a Princess; by a series of "chances" Lord Radstock was unexpectedly with the Princess when the Grand Duchess was announced. And after her conversion she invited him to Russia.

The great writer Dostoievsky heard Radstock preach in 1873. "I found nothing startling", he wrote in his *Diary of a Writer* (1876). "He spoke neither particularly cleverly nor in a particularly dull manner. But yet he performs miracles over human hearts; people are flocking around him, many of them are astounded; they are looking for the poor, in order as quickly as possible to bestow benefits upon them; they are almost ready to give away their fortunes . . . He does produce extraordinary transformations and inspires in the hearts of his followers magnanimous sentiments."

Brobrinsky's palace and his country estates, like those of Paschkoff and other converts, became centres of the new evangelical movement and models of agricultural and humane reform. The Revival went from strength to strength. Lord Radstock, whose Russian was not fluent enough for preaching, worked in the drawing rooms and his converts went out among the poorer classes. New Testaments, almost unknown to the ordinary Russian, were distributed in tens of thousands from the Neva and the Vistula to prison camps in Siberia. Prayer meetings began in place after place.

The Radstock revival had incalculable possibilities for Russia. Many of the educated classes were intensely religious yet unsatisfied by the detached formalism which encrusted the Orthodox Church; they were intensely patriotic yet disturbed by Russia's monolithic, repressive political system and by "the segregation", as Dostoievsky called it, "of the educated strata of society, our detachment from our own soil, from the nation". The evangelical revival could have done much to end this fatal detachment, for nobles and *muzhiks* met as brothers. Here was a better road than that of Nihilist revolutionaries.

But the wrath of the Russian Orthodox Church was aroused. What might have been a reformation within the Church was forced to be a sect outside it; the informal groups of all classes which gathered round Paschkoff, Brobrinsky and other friends of Lord Radstock in St Petersburg and in their country estates, became known as "Evangelical Christians". Leadership lay with nobles and gentry, and at first they were protected by their position. "Leave my widows alone!" the Tsar replied when church authorities wished to proceed against Princess Lieven, in whose palace the St Petersburg Evangelical Christians held their services.

In 1881 Alexander II was blown to pieces by a Nihilist bomb. He had been on the verge of granting a further measure of political freedom and religious toleration. His son Alexander III answered his father's murder by stark reaction.

.   .   .   .   .   .

In 1884 Colonel Paschkoff convened a united evangelical conference, and some four hundred converged on St Petersburg. He hired a hotel and gave them hospitality, having already paid their fares. They met in a hall in Princess Lieven's palace where every servant was a convert except the surly old *dvornik* or doorkeeper, and represented the three major strands of Russian evangelicalism, the Baptists, the Evangelical Christians, and the Stundists. These were a sect which had arisen when Russian peasants had attended (illegally) the *stunden* or Bible hours conducted by evangelical German farmers in the Ukraine, who had been given liberty of worship when invited to settle but were forbidden to proselytize.

Each strand was of different origin, but a classic example of the spontaneous expansion of the Church: Christians from another nation had touched off a movement which propagated itself, thoroughly indigenous in leadership and character. The three movements, unrelated yet emerging almost simultaneously, affected North and South, the illiterate peasants, the merchants, the nobility. This evangelical revival, widespread, gathering momentum, might have changed the course of Russian history.

The conference of 1884 continued happily for three or four days. On the next, no provincial delegate appeared. Princess Lieven, Colonel Paschkoff and their aristocratic allies were puzzled by the disappearance of these men far from their homes. The hotel was empty. Two days later a scared *muzhik* delegate slipped into the palace. He told how they had been arrested shortly after leaving the conference. In the fortress of St Peter and St

Paul they had been searched and questioned. Some of them were told that revolutionary literature had been seized from the others, at which they laughed. "The only revolutionary document possessed or used by any of us is the Bible! We aim at no revolution other than that which the Cross of our Lord Jesus Christ effects."

Police had escorted them to railway stations for despatch home at government expense; the *muzhik* who gave the news to Paschkoff had cannily asked for a ticket to a place near St Petersburg and had doubled back at risk of arrest and punishment.

The collapse of the conference was a prelude to an intense and violent persecution in which Church and State vied to suppress the evangelicals. Princess Lieven had to retire to her estates. Paschkoff was banished. When, on petition to the Tsar, he was allowed a brief return to settle his affairs, Alexander III soon peremptorily ordered him to private audience.

"I hear you have resumed your old practices!"

"My friends have certainly called to greet me, and we have prayed and read the Word of God together . . ."

"Which you know perfectly well I will not permit. I will not have you defy me. If I had thought you would repeat your offences I should not have allowed you to return. Get out. And never set foot in Russia again."

No such mild fate awaited the majority of the evangelical leaders. They were harried, persecuted, imprisoned, exiled to Siberia, Transcaucasia or other barren confines of the Empire. Not being men of rank, they were treated as any criminals – beards and hair half-shaved, wrists and ankles shackled by heavy chains – they were driven across mountains and deserts beside bandits, swindlers and rapists. They suffered worse than Lenin and most revolutionaries whose exile was unmarred by flogging, hard labour or the treadmill. Their wives would have been destitute without the charity of their fellow believers; when a man's sentence was served he would be kept in exile by administrative order and his family could sometimes join him – travelling under such inhumane conditions that women and children often died on the road.

Faith was bent and tested. That of a few broke. That of most proved gloriously resilient. "How good the Lord is", exclaimed Paschkoff's Inspector of Forest at the start of the march to Siberia. "I have been praying to work among the prisoners and this is how my prayer is answered."

.   .   .   .   .

"Radstockism", as its detractors called the movement, was sent underground. But if in England the Methodist Revival prevented revolution in 1789, the Evangelical Revival of the eighteen seventies, had it been allowed to take its course, might have so purified Russian life and government that the revolution of 1917, with all the misery that Communism brought the world, would never have occurred. God gave Russia her opportunity, and His Wesley was Lord Radstock.

Excluded from Russia, Radstock's work was not done. In Sweden, Denmark, Finland, and often in

Paris, now republican and bitter in defeat, he moved quietly among both upper classes and the poor. Seven times he went to India, and in 1897 he organized a scheme by which every native official received a New Testament on Queen Victoria's Jubilee.

At home, news of his work in Russia opened doors hitherto closed among the aristocracy of England; his ambition to reach his own class was rewarded, though without spectacular results. And scarcely an evangelical work or mission was untouched by him. For over thirty· years, almost to the Great War, his name crosses and recrosses the story of England's religious movements. The Cambridge Seven were influenced by him; he helped Moody and Sankey, and Torrey and Alexander; man after man on the mission field or in home service could point to some moment when an address or a personal word from Radstock changed the course of their lives.

The missionary to Imperial Russia died in December 1913, little more than three years before the Russian Revolution.

His movement, however, did not die.

When Lenin separated the Orthodox Church from the state, and all sects were briefly allowed freedom to worship and evangelize, the three evangelical strands, united as "The Evangelical Christians/Baptists", experienced great growth. Then the Soviet Union attempted to extinguish religion and promote militant atheism. A violent persecution swept across the land. Thousands of Christians of all churches were killed, or suffered hardship, torture and hunger in labour camps, until Stalin at length restored a small measure of religious freedom during the Second

World War, followed by further restriction under Khrushchev.

The Orthodox Church had been purged as by fire, and now saw the evangelicals as brothers in Christ. As one archbishop said to me, deep in Soviet Central Asia at the height of the Khrushchev repression: "Once we chased them with a pitchfork; now we draw them to us with a kiss of peace."

Through all the slander and persecution the Christians loved their enemies and prayed for those who despitefully used them. When restrictions were again eased, while the spiritual bankruptcy of atheism, and of Communism, became yearly more obvious, the evangelists were already showing a better way by the purity of their motives and the beauty of their lives. Thus they were a strong component of the Russian religious revival of the later twentieth century.

The Soviet state at last admitted, in 1989, that the attempt to abolish religion had been wrong. The church bells rang again; Christian services and preachers were seen and heard on state television; evangelists were allowed to use stadiums.

The Evangelical Christians/Baptists were ready to help the nation into paths of righteousness, because the Lord was indeed their Shepherd. Thus Lord Radstock's greatest harvest began to be reaped three-quarters of a century after his death.

Like all in this book he had sowed in love and faith. As Mary Slessor had said, "God and one is a majority".